Praise for Margaret Mitchell's No Laughing Matter

"This is more than a memoir of an individual life, but the memoir of a nation. Mitchell's personal experiences—from her life in small town Ontario . . . to her political activism and accomplishments as a social worker and Member of Parliament—are a call for us to build upon the efforts of her pioneering life."

—Cynthia E. Milton, Canada Research Chair
Department of History, Université de Montréal
author of The Many Meanings of Poverty

"No Laughing Matter brings to life some of the rich, historic community development initiatives that Margaret pioneered in Vancouver. Her stories show how, as a community social worker, she helped local people to use their collective power to solve local issues. There are many lessons here for volunteers, academics, social reformers and the like who are passionate about building strong communities. No Laughing Matter is a positive energizer for everyone who needs a beacon in their struggle for progressive social change."

—Roopchand B. Seebaran, Professor Emeritus
School of Social Work, University of British Columbia

"Mitchell is one of Vancouver's civic treasures, and the city owes her a great debt. Her behind-the-scenes grassroots work helped build Vancouver into the livable, multi-cultural city that it is today. This book will be a key text for planners, social workers, community workers and social justice activists."

—Jo-Anne Lee, Associate Professor
Dept. of Women's Studies
University of Victoria

"Margaret's book is a very interesting personal journey. It brought back many happy memories of our times in Korea, Japan, Australia and Mayne Island, B.C."

—Pam (Whitehead) MacLeod,
family friend

Net proceeds from the sale of No Laughing Matter will be donated to the Margaret Mitchell Fund for Women, held and managed by the Vancity Community Foundation.

In 1980, Member of Parliament Margaret Mitchell refused a pay raise and set up a holding account for the excess money. In 1997, she gave the accumulated monies to the Vancity Community Foundation to establish a fund to empower women in her constituency. Women living in the riding of Vancouver East can apply for scholarships and self-help programs to the Margaret Mitchell Fund for Women.

For more information or to donate please call 604-877-7647 or email vcf@vancity.com

Suzanne —

Welcome to Vancouver

Margaret.

No Laughing Matter

Adventure, Activism and Politics

by Margaret Mitchell

Granville Island Publishing

Library and Archives Canada Cataloguing in Publication

Mitchell, Margaret A., 1925-

    No laughing matter : adventure, activism & politics / Margaret A. Mitchell.

Includes bibliographical references and index.

ISBN 978-1-894694-63-6

1. Mitchell, Margaret A., 1925–. 2. Canada. Parliament. House of Commons— Biography. 3. Legislators—Canada—Biography. 4. Women political activists— Canada—Biography. 5. British Columbia—Biography. 6. Vancouver (B.C.)— Biography. 7. New Democratic Party—Biography.
I. Title.

FC3847.26.M48A3 2007   971.1'3304092   C2007-906436-1

Editor: Lauren Ollsin
Proofreader: Neall Calvert
Indexer: bookmark: editing & indexing
Front cover photo: Photo Features Ltd.
Designer: Rebecca Davies Design

All efforts have been made to contact photographers for their permission to print photographs. If you are one of these, please contact the publisher.

Granville Island Publishing Ltd.
212–1656 Duranleau St · Granville Island
Vancouver BC · Canada · V6H 3S4
info@granvilleislandpublishing.com

First Published January 2008 • Printed in Canada

DEDICATION

I dedicate this book to young women
who want to make a difference.

Margaret Mitchell

CONTENTS

SECTION 2: COMMUNITY DEVELOPMENT

SECTION 3: POLITICS

ACKNOWLEDGEMENTS

Finally this 80-year story is written! It began in Ontario in the 1920s, but the writing started in the 1950s in the form of letters and diaries documenting my adventures in the Far East, Australia, and Vienna. My fading memory was spiked by my husband Claude's many stories, my writings on community development, and parliamentary documents, which were useful for subsequent chapters.

There are so many people to acknowledge that I decided a list was needed. I want particularly to thank:

Lil Reid Smith—the boss of my constituency
    office (and me) for fourteen years
Patsy George—faithful supporter through social
    work, community development, and politi-
    cal times
Crissy George (Patsy's sister) and our many mutual
    friends, who often were manuscript readers
My NDP sisters—Audrey McLaughlin, Lynn
    Hunter, Dawn Black, and Darlene Marzari
My two patient editors—Ellen Shultze and
    Lauren Ollsin

In absentia:
My partner, Claude Mitchell—Aussie jokester and
    my constant supporter until death
My sister, Betty Speers (and her family)—friend
    and travel mate
Pauline Jewett—my MP mate
Doris Anderson—encourager and reader of first
    drafts

PROLOGUE

"No Laughing Matter"

Political notoriety came my way in 1982 when a single incident in the House of Commons made me furious, and famous. The Trudeau Liberals held sway in Ottawa and I was NDP Member of Parliament for Vancouver East. I had worked for months with the combined Standing Committees on Health and Welfare and Justice, hearing from many witnesses of the suffering battered women were experiencing, the lack of safe refuge for abused women and their children, and of a justice system which had not only failed to protect them but which had also failed to prosecute offenders. On May 12th I rose in the House to raise the urgent need for government action on a serious and widespread issue.

"The parliamentary report on battered wives states that one in ten Canadian husbands beat their wives regularly," I began. Before I could continue, an uproar of male shouts and laughter erupted, making it impossible for me to be heard. A nearby Tory joked, "I don't beat my wife. Do you, George?"

When the Speaker finally got order, I rose again in fury. "Madam Speaker, I do not think this is a laughing matter. What action will the Minister responsible for the Status of Women undertake immediately at the federal level to protect battered women?" I demanded. "I want action, not just reports, research, and conferences."

The Minister responsible, the Honourable Judy Erola, replied that she, too, did not find the men's derision amusing, "and neither do the women of Canada." Her solution was to increase the number of transition houses under the Canada Assistance Plan, passing responsibility back to the provinces.

Not to be deterred, I informed the Solicitor General that out of 10,000 incidents of violence, only two offenders were convicted. "Will he take action to require that the federal courts and law enforcement agencies treat assault as a criminal offence?" I asked. "Will he also intensify training programs for the RCMP and other police so that they will enforce the law to protect battered women?"

My angry questions topped the TV news that evening. The uproarious and outrageous response by many male MPs (several of whom were rumoured to be batterers) sent shock waves across the country, awakening Canadians to the severity of violence against women and to the callous attitude of many male parliamentarians. The next morning I asked for all-party support for a motion calling for an apology from the House. Some MPs refused, defeating my motion.

Women's groups across the country rallied. They mounted a major protest, helping to raise awareness of violence against women among politicians and the general public. In the months to come, both federal and provincial governments responded with progressive change. RCMP and local police forces trained officers to respond to domestic violence, and more charges were laid. More funds were allocated to establish transition houses for women to escape violent partners and find new circumstances. Educational programs made the public more aware that violence was not to be tolerated.

Ironically, this accidental incident became my claim to fame. The video footage of my question in the House, which had become a classic, was used in workshops on family violence and on TV programs dealing with the subject. And for years afterward, women told me that that incident in the House of Commons had helped them gain the confidence to escape from violent situations. In 2002, I was a special guest at a symposium celebrating the twentieth anniversary of this event and the societal change it had initiated. One woman called it "a turning point in feminism in Canada."

So how did a shy young woman who grew up in a small, conservative Ontario town end up as an active socialist and an advocate for women in the House of Commons? It was the result of some 25 years of changes, experience overseas, and maturing. Unlike many who enter politics, I didn't grow up in a political family, and certainly not a socialist one. Our roots and relatives were middle class, which in our family meant church-going Protestants with a tradition of conformity, helping others, and strong family ties. In keeping with that tradition, we didn't talk politics at home. When I asked Dad about his own politics, he said he always voted for "the man." Later, I noted that "the man" was always a Conservative. On the other hand, Mother's sister, my Aunt Hilda, wasn't reticent about talking politics, although she demonstrated her flexible political leanings when she couldn't decide who should get her vote— Handsome "Commie" Tim Buck, or Handsome "Tory" George Drew. I inherited a sense of community that was to lead to political action in later life.

SECTION 1

Early Adventures

CHAPTER ONE

Growing Up: Childhood in Cayuga, Ontario

My father, Clarence Learoyd, was born at the end of the 1800s, during Queen Victoria's reign. He came from a long line of ministers who had immigrated to Canada from Yorkshire, England, in the early 1800s. Although my memories of my grandparents are sketchy, I remember Grandma Learoyd as a strong personality who passed along her very clear sense of right and wrong to our family. Dad, the eldest of four children, rejected the ministry for teaching, as did his sister Alma and brother Everett. Their youngest brother, Harold, became a dentist.

My mother, Ernestine Dutton, was five years younger than Dad. Her family came from Chester, England. Although I know little else about them, I do know that one of her relatives was descended from United Empire Loyalists who came to Canada after the American Revolution. Mother's parents died early, and she and her sister, Hilda, who was teaching in Fort William (now Thunder Bay), were guardians of their younger brother, Lawrason. He lived with my parents during his teenage years after his parents (my grandparents) died.

Dad met Mother in Fort William, where he was teaching after having graduated from the University of Toronto. Although Mother trained as a nurse, she had to give up nursing due to her own poor health, but not before she had received an award—which we still have—for the care she gave patients during the great flu epidemic of 1918. Mother and Dad were married in 1922 in Brockville, Ontario.

I was born in 1925, the second of four children spaced two years apart. My older brother, Bill, my younger brother, Ted, and I were born in Brockville, and then Betty, the baby, was born after the family moved to Cayuga. It was a pretty rural town of close to 800, located on the Grand River, about 30 kilometres southwest of Hamilton, where Dad would be high-school principal for 30 years.

Although my parents provided the love, security and encouragement that helped me to develop a strong personality, family stresses took their toll when we four children were mostly preschoolers. Our mother was taken away from us in a traumatic fashion. She was hospitalized for tuberculosis, and became one of the guinea pigs for the pneumo-thorax operation, which slashed her body from neck to tailbone, removing one lung and several ribs. Except for one short period at home, she spent the next four years in Hamilton's Mountain Sanatorium. How heartbreaking it must have been for a woman like her with such a young family. Dad took us to the hospital to visit her, but we could only wave from the grounds below. I longed for my mother, but didn't really get to know her until she came home when I was six. I still remember the beautiful embroidered dresses she made for Betty and me and the sweaters she knitted during that time.

While Mother was hospitalized, I was shipped to Toronto to stay with my Uncle Everett's family and attend kindergarten at the school where he taught. On weekends I stayed with my Aunt Alma, who spoiled me. I loved staying there. I especially remember her being a loving nurse when I was ill with the measles and confined to a dark room.

During the years when Mother was away, we all coped as best we could. My older brother, Bill, was attending school. Ted lived on a farm with friends of Mother's, and our housekeeper raised Betty. We each seemed to find a substitute mother. In my case it was my music teacher. She provided much-needed support over the six or seven years when I was learning to play the piano and organ. I remember her cookies and hugs, but I think our relationship was diminished somewhat in later years when I blanked out on Beethoven and failed my Grade VIII Royal Conservatory of Toronto piano exam!

Those years when Mother was hospitalized were difficult for all of us, but especially for Dad. He carried a heavy load teaching in an understaffed school, managing motherless children at home with the help of a housekeeper, and doing his school work late into the night. Twice a week, he drove the 30 kilometres to Hamilton to visit Mother. He was perpetually tired. One time, he went to sleep at the wheel and was almost killed when he hit a concrete post.

Despite his workload, Dad found time for us. I remember a daylong journey we took to Niagara Falls and the exciting sky-car trip over the rapids. When she heard about the trip, Mother was horrified that her little darlings had been at risk. When Dad drove us to Lake Erie for a swim or for camping, we competed in singing out, "I see the lake, I see the lake," whether we saw it or not. We felt lucky to have a car with a horn that sounded "Cayuga."

After two stints in Hamilton Mountain TB Sanatorium, Mother returned home and began a new relationship with her young family. Life as we knew it was changing again. And although she needed some help around the house, she still cooked and canned and sewed our clothes and kept us up to Cayuga social standards. Her friends always praised her for being a wonderful homemaker. In deference to her health, we were quiet each afternoon so that she could have a nap (a practice we all adopted later in life too).

It was clear that Mother loved Dad, and I never heard them quarrel (this would not have been proper in front of the kids), but my parents were quite different in their approaches to life. Mother was a conscientious and serious person. Although she wasn't snobbish, social status was important to her. She liked to think that she was part of the middle class. She was concerned about our social circle, and encouraged us in music and other cultural pursuits. She and Dad played bridge with the school inspector and his wife, and Mother socialized with other middle-class neighbours. Dad related to everyone.

From Mother, I learned my homemaking skills and feminine interests—clothes, decorating, cooking, and entertaining—but I inherited Dad's egalitarian values and his enjoyment of people. Dad was more outgoing than Mom, with a lively sense of humour and a strong sense of community. He treated all people equally, including the three black families in town, and he had a special sensitivity to farm families.

Although Mother and Dad had their differences, they shared a strong sense of social values and community responsibility. Our parents went to church regularly and we kids went to Sunday school, but religion played a relatively minor role in our family. As in most small towns, the church in Cayuga also served as a social hub. I sang in the choir, and was a member of CGIT. However, religion did have a negative effect on my relationship with one of my siblings, my older brother, Bill. In our early days he was a fun-loving fellow who eagerly took part in shenanigans, which often involved the two of us teasing our younger brother Ted or playing music together. I was embarrassed and disappointed when he changed from being my chum into an evangelist and began to proselytize both at school and at home. His attempts to convert me turned me off religion altogether.

The Great Depression affected everyone, and the members of our family were no exception. Fortunately Dad and Mother were very good financial managers; their thrift influenced my later attitudes to consumerism and spending. Recycling was essential and nothing was wasted. Although Dad's salary was minimal, we survived those years with mother's ingenuity, a large garden and the income from the summer jobs Dad took on (marking exams, soil sampling, or labouring). We loved to play with the angora rabbits that Dad raised for fur and meat. There was no money for clothes or for presents other than the ones our parents made themselves, but every week they paid something to the hospital towards my mother's medical bills (there was no Medicare in those days). Despite our precarious financial circumstances, we shared what we had. Unemployed "hoboes" who were riding the rails often stopped at our house to ask for something to eat in exchange for doing odd jobs. They were never turned away. And every Sunday, a dollar went into the collection envelope, half for the missionaries in China—it was always China—and half for the church.

Even though our parents never worried us kids about finances, I was always aware that money was tight. We learned to budget, and to share the workload of running the household. We all had chores. We washed dishes, tidied up, and as we got older, pumped water to the cistern in the attic of our square, four-storey house. For our efforts we received a small weekly allowance (ten cents), which was increased annually by five cents.

Despite financial constraints and the absence of my mother during my early years, by and large I had a normal childhood. My close friend Dot Schweyer and I played house, picked wild strawberries in the spring, gathered hickory nuts in the fall, and went to school together. I remember once being frightened by a grade-school teacher who warned us that if we didn't behave, she would "throw us out the window and listen to us bounce." We behaved.

In summer, Dot and I joined the neighbourhood boys on forays to steal juicy watermelons. In winter we skated on the creek (pronounced 'crick') and roasted potatoes over a campfire. I don't recall Mother trying to curtail my activities, but she used to ask, "Why don't you invite the kids up here to play?" She couldn't understand why we ignored her invitation, but for me it was because it was too polite and clean at our house for us to have fun. And of course Dad was a teacher, which also had a dampening effect.

The fun and friendliness of a small town where everyone knew and accepted you, and the many community activities influenced my love of community, which later led me to a community development career. In Cayuga, the ice rink was the centre of winter activities. In the summer, "Saturday Night Sports," a program of street activities, drew shoppers from nearby areas during the Depression. We kids had a wonderful time racing, dancing, flirting and getting into mischief.

Adolescence and Wartime

When I got a little older, my closest friends were Gloria and Pat Thurston, the youngest children in a large Irish Canadian family. Their mother had died before they came to town and their father eked out a living for the family in his shoe repair shop. The siblings raised each other, and two of the older sisters worked in turn as our 'hired girls.' Although their home was built only from lightweight crating materials, it was always filled with fun and laughter.

As time went on, Pat and Gloria and I began to go our separate ways. They were beautiful girls and had boyfriends. I was shy with boys and discouraged the few who were courageous enough to make overtures. Sex remained an intriguing mystery. On one occasion I begged my mother to let me go with my friends to a dance in a nearby town. Reluctantly she agreed, but I was a miserable wallflower for the whole evening. Sexual maturity seemed to come later to me than to other girls. Inhibitions that held me back no doubt began in childhood. Mother prepared me for adolescence by giving me a book about menstruation, but she never got around to talking about sex. Sex was a taboo word in my family. It was certainly never considered an activity that people actually engaged in—even fun-loving Aunt Hilda was quiet on this subject. It wasn't until I was at summer camp, which I loved, that a wonderful Camp Mother filled the gap for me by explaining intercourse as part of a loving relationship.

As a teenager, my relationship with my mother grew closer and my relationship with my father more ambivalent. In high school I loved to cut up in class to prove I was not the teacher's pet. On one occasion this earned me a trip to the principal's (my father's) office, and chastisement both there and at home. Although Dad pretended to be a tough disciplinarian, he enjoyed his students (when he wasn't exhausted) and joked about their antics. I resented this double standard. When I complained that I wasn't allowed to be like the other kids, Mother understood, and persuaded Dad to let me play hooky occasionally with my friends. I also remember Mother chastised Dad once for not attending a piano recital in which I was a lead performer. He attended my recitals after that.

Although I did well in school and showed natural leadership there, I learned humility from Dad early in life. It remained a lifetime characteristic not common in politicians. Dad was not one to praise, but when he gave me a pat, I knew he was pleased with me. Mother encouraged a more direct approach. I remember her saying to him, "Why can't you tell her she did a good job?" On the other hand, if I misbehaved at home, he sometimes gave me a flick on the ear, which was more humiliating than painful. The strap was reserved for the boys.

Perhaps the strongest influence on me while I was growing up was my father's philosophy and forward thinking. He wrote the following excerpt for the December 4, 1935 issue of the Cayuga High School newspaper. It reflected his views on citizenship, which influenced my later decision to become a social worker and politician.

It is not for your own sake that you are now going to school. You are soon to become a more active citizen of Canada. You will require more than book knowledge and culture. In school you must aim to cultivate those virtues which will make you unselfish, law abiding, and willing to help in every good enterprise. Can you think of any way in which you can assist the activities of your school or help your fellow pupils? Then act on the first good impulse. Intelligent and willing co-operation is a mark of a good citizenship. It is more important that you should become a good citizen than that you achieve high honours or personal gain. Be courteous, honest, industrious and self-reliant. Learn to help yourself, that you may help others.

My father wasn't the only one in the family to hold this view of helping others. One of the most constant influences on our young lives was the love and generosity shown to us by our two 'maiden' aunts, Alma and Hilda. Years later, I realized that when I was with my sister Betty's kids, I was repeating the role of the loving and giving aunt that both Aunt Hilda and Aunt Alma had played in our family.

When Mother was in hospital, the aunts took turns visiting us on weekends and often had us visit them in Toronto. Both were teachers who loved to travel, but there the similarity ended. Dad's sister, Alma, was the true daughter of a minister, always helping others, with a strict moral code which she did not impose, but you always knew she was there watching. Aunt Alma had inherited the family home in Toronto and happily housed elderly relatives who needed a place to live. Later, three of us kids lived with her while we attended university, for which she also supplied loans. Betty, who became a nurse, received help for travel from Aunt Alma, and also lived with her on one occasion.

Aunt Hilda Dutton, Mother's sister, was the jolly aunt. She was direct and full of humour and inclined to take a nip or a smoke when Aunt Alma was not around. Aunt Hilda taught art and in later years became a prolific artist. It was Aunt Hilda who encouraged Betty and me to be adventurous. She often talked to us about going west to work, which ultimately we both did. One summer Aunt Hilda drove us in her new car to see the famous "Quints," the Dionne quintuplets. The five little girls were kept in a fenced-in home where the public could view them.

I thought that they were cute but wondered if they liked being stared at like animals in a zoo.

Looking back, I think that my Aunt Hilda and my Aunt Alma were the role models who led me to a life of independence and travel. Even though I had a traditional family upbringing, I was given freedom and encouraged to try new things. My family's encouragement led to a desire for change, and an enthusiasm for adventure. On one occasion during my teens, this manifested itself in a bicycle trip through the tobacco-growing area of southern Ontario with a girlfriend, with my parents' reluctant permission.

As far back as I can remember, we girls were expected to be independent. Both Betty and I were encouraged to take up a career. Being part of the working world was not only a necessity, it was expected of us. However, we were not expected to conform to the norm of getting married at an early age, and I suspect my avoidance of sex and my late marriage also may have resulted from the strong influence of Aunt Alma and Aunt Hilda.

Our world changed when war was declared in 1939. My brother Bill joined the Army Medical Corps. Those of us at home knitted for the Red Cross and wrote to soldiers. I also became an enthusiastic member of the Farmerette Corps, working three summers on farms near Waterford and in the Niagara Peninsula. Farmerettes provided government-sponsored wartime labour for farmers. We were billeted in high-school dorms and picked up by the farmers each morning. We earned 25 cents a day.

Being a Farmerette was hard work, but I enjoyed making many new friends and I learned a lot about farming. We hoed fields, stooked grain, and picked tobacco, okra, and fruits. Unfortunately, I also learned that showing off could have unexpectedly painful and long-term consequences. This was brought home to me one threshing day when there were a lot of people around, including the farmer's attractive young sons. With this illustrious audience, I decided to slide down a straw stack which was taller than the farmer's barn.

What had looked like a safe, natural slope down, wasn't. I dropped straight onto my tail-bone, injuring my back quite badly. I was in a lot of pain, but tried to hide it. I was embarrassed by my own foolishness, and kept on working, moving heavy grain bags. I never did see a doctor, and my back was injured for life. As I grew older, I suffered from back and leg pains, which I still experience today.

Leaving Home—McMaster University

My last years in high school were lonely because all my close friends had boyfriends and several quit school. The war was on, and only one boy remained in our Grade 13 class when I was valedictorian. I wasn't sure what I wanted to do after graduation.

Mother eventually persuaded me to enrol at McMaster, a small university in Hamilton. I would live in residence and have more opportunity for a livelier social life. My two aunts provided loans for my fees, but since there was little money for clothes, Mother made me two suits from men's clothes. This wasn't ideal, but I knew it was all we could afford.

I was excited to be going to university and looked forward to the opening ceremonies. Because the women's residence was crowded, five of us shared a room meant for three. We were all from different parts of Ontario, and became close friends.

When I had decided to go to university, I knew I wanted to work with people but I had no specific career in mind. I chose the social service option because it combined the subjects that interested me—sociology, psychology, anthropology and English. Volunteer work at a crisis clinic stimulated my interest in social work but I knew I could not afford two more years for postgraduate studies. To earn extra cash, I took on a job making sandwiches. I kept up my studies but also learned to enjoy occasional parties and dances.

Work had always played an important role in my life, whether it was chores I did as a child or farm work during war years. Each job taught me something, and the job I had waiting on tables at Bigwin Inn in Muskoka for two summers during my undergraduate years was no exception. It was there that I had my first experience with overt racism. I was shocked when the German head waitress placed lunch guests with Jewish names at the worst tables, after long waits. I later learned that no Jewish guests were accepted at Bigwin. I learned another lesson when I returned home with Bigwin "souvenirs." Mother insisted I return them, with an apology. That was the first and last time I "lifted" memorabilia.

Although going to university had certainly expanded my social horizon, I didn't have a wild social life at McMaster even though dances and parties and university events provided diversion. Since our family encouraged independence, making a living, and travel, I didn't consider dating and romance to be important. I wasn't looking for a husband, but I did go out with a couple of guys during my university years. John came to visit me at Bigwin and we dated occasionally. Later Keith became my regular date for university events, and he continued to visit me in Toronto while I was attending graduate school. I still had not fallen in love, but my sociology prof in a red gown who taught the popular Sex 30 class looked pretty sexy, and so did the older returning vets who swelled the Mac population, making it a more dynamic place and diminishing its Baptist traditions.

During my second year at McMaster, my life changed dramatically. I was called to the Hamilton hospital where my Mother, who had only one lung, now had pneumonia. When I went to visit her she was not very strong, but she was talking, and I could see that she was worried. She looked very discouraged, and I imagine she was envisaging another lengthy stay in hospital because she asked me about finances. (This was before Canada had Medicare coverage.) "Do you think that maybe we could accept government help this time?" she asked apologetically. I assured her that of course we could, even though this was completely contrary to my parents' philosophy of independence. My awareness of the need for Medicare began at this time.

A few minutes later, Mother just drifted away. I thought she had fainted and called the nurse in a panic, pleading with her to revive my mother. I was frantic. She hadn't been sick that long, and it hadn't appeared to be serious. But it was. The doctor told me she was dead. I phoned Dad and my aunts, but I was so upset I could hardly talk. I could not believe that the mother I loved and relied on was gone. This was my first experience with death.

I was devastated. I don't think anyone saw this coming. It had been quite some time since Mother had been in hospital. I was at university, Bill was in the army, and Ted was also living away from home. Besides Dad, only Betty was left at home. She was fifteen, and although I don't remember her complaining, this was a pretty unhappy time for her.

I must have been in shock at the time because I do not remember much from that period in my life. Bill came home from the army, and my Aunt Hilda and my Aunt Alma were a great support to all of us. Many Cayuga people attended Mother's funeral. She was well respected and loved.

Although we had had a housekeeper while Mother was alive, after she died, Dad asked Betty if she would rather have an allowance to do the work herself. She chose to do the work, but it wasn't much fun, and I don't imagine Dad was very good company at the time, either.

I have always felt guilty about that period in my life. I returned to McMaster where studies, dances, bridge and other diversions eased my depression. It was during this time that I learned to fence, something I only pursued later when I wanted to show off. I probably didn't get home as often as I should have, leaving Dad and Betty to cope with their loneliness by themselves. When I did make the bus trip home every two or three weeks, the three of us were faced with the big hole Mother's death had left in all of our lives.

Moving On—University of Toronto School of Social Work

After completing my undergraduate degree at McMaster, I went to work in the dress department at Eaton's department store in Toronto to earn some money. I was living with Aunt Alma, who was also housing two elderly relatives. This was the year of the long skirt, which I had to wear for my job as a store clerk. While I was working there, I learned one invaluable fashion lesson: how to dress up my one dark dress with dazzling multicoloured scarves. By fall I had decided to enrol in the University of Toronto's School of Social Work.

It was during my time at U of T that I began to take my first fledgling steps towards politics. I became aware of social needs and of progressive social policy. I joined the fledgling Student Union and was influenced by many Jewish students who were politically active. I opposed injustices and wanted social change. My emotions and horizons were broadening to the political left.

My changing view also influenced my choice of Group Work rather than Case Work as my area of Social Work specialization. I enjoyed being with groups and organizing activities, and I was drawn to the strong focus on reform exhibited by the School of Social Work under the leadership of Dr. Harry Cassidy. Cassidy had initiated welfare reform in British Columbia, and was an advisor to the federal government. He was an outstanding man who influenced many people even as he was dying of cancer. Another strong influence on my work was the head of Group Work, Professor Alan Klein. He was an American lawyer who introduced us to social action and multiculturalism. I learned a lot about group process, which could be applied in many settings to promote growth, solve problems, and to educate. Both men were influential in developing my interest in social action.

Two days a week were dedicated to the field-work aspect of my studies. My supervisor, Giff Gifford, was a socialist who later organized Veterans for Peace. I worked at Central Neighbourhood House in Toronto's "Cabbage Town," helping young children benefit from the "group process." I particularly enjoyed working with groups of young girls. I liked the approach of the Neighbourhood Houses, which followed the examples set by "settlement houses" in England. Programmes focused on families, especially single mothers, for whom poverty was a daily concern.

The kids we worked with were quite deprived. They came from a fairly depressed area of Toronto. Through group activities and the relationships we developed, we were helping them to change behaviour and become more socialized. I remember one little girl who posed a particular challenge. She was totally deaf and had a very explosive temper as a result of her frustration. While we were trying to prepare a special Christmas program, she always disrupted the group. Even though she couldn't hear the music, I made her the lead fairy in "The Sugarplum Fairy." She was pleased and co-operative, and I was delighted by her progress.

During the summer I worked with Alan Klein and two of my pals at Camp Winnebago, a Jewish camp, where we applied Group Work in a community setting. Armed with new insight, I was beginning to develop my own approach to social work. In my second year I did my field work at the YWCA and began work on my thesis, "Group Work – Case Work Collaboration." I documented experiences in several settings where group workers and case workers collaborated to serve people more effectively. Three years later, one day before the deadline, it was finished and I received my Master of Social Work degree. I negotiated a union wage with the Toronto YWCA and for five years was a program director in two of its branches.

These should have been exciting times for me, but they weren't. I worked most evenings, had very little social life, and lived with girlfriends in crowded apartments. One place we lived in was near Yonge Street, close to where they were building the subway. I was awakened by the pile drivers every morning. We were all saving money (in my case to pay back Aunt Alma), so our apartment housed more people than there were beds. Nurses on night shift shared the bed with those who worked days. The beds rarely cooled off.

Finally I paid off my debt to Aunt Alma and was ready for new experiences. One summer, five of us drove across Canada and the US, but that only whetted my appetite for more travel and adventure. I was feeling depressed and bored with my job. Fortunately, in 1953, the promise of new horizons came in the form of a job offer. Dr. Chick Hendry, Director of the University of Toronto School of Social Work, recommended me for an overseas posting with the Canadian Red Cross as a welfare worker with the Commonwealth Armed Forces in Japan. A new and exciting phase in my life was about to begin.

Although I couldn't have known it at the time, accepting the Red Cross posting in Japan was an important turning point in my life. It was the first link in a chain of events that would ultimately lead me to the House of Commons. Along the way, I would fulfill a long-time dream of travelling in Australia's Outback, and meet the man I would later marry—the first person to recognize that I had the potential to be a successful politician. Taking that first step into overseas work also prepared me to work in Vienna with refugees from the Hungarian Revolution. It was there that I began to question the accepted role of social work in Canadian society and to consider a new approach to problem solving: community development. And it was my work in community development that gave me the insight and exposure that ultimately enabled me to run successfully for elected office in Vancouver East.

The road from rural Ontario to the House of Commons was not without bumps and curves, but the strengths, values and sense of community that I developed with the help of my extended family during my childhood in Cayuga gave me the determination to tackle the many challenges I encountered along the way.

CHAPTER 2

The Korean War, Japan and the International Red Cross

I sank into my seat on a plane headed from Vancouver over the Aleutians to Japan. It was 1953. I was 28, and had been recruited by the Canadian Red Cross to serve with the Commonwealth Forces in Japan and Korea. This was my first trip overseas. As I slowly relaxed after a hectic week of preparations, I wondered what experiences lay ahead.

What a change it would be from the female environment of the YWCA and the lonely life I had been leading. When the unexpected call came from the Red Cross, it took me one minute to decide to join their Far East team.

I had no idea how much and in what ways this decision would change my life. It would lead to intense new experiences, lifetime friendships, cultural immersion and first-hand views of the military environment in postwar Japan. I would be one of only a few women in a world of men with postings in hospitals and leave centres in Japan, and in a "MASH"-like field dressing station and a front-line recreation centre in Korea. I would become a lifetime pacifist, opposing war.

I was joining a civilian team of Red Cross welfare workers attached to British Commonwealth Forces. A truce in the Korean War was imminent, and Red Cross workers were being assigned to work with Canadian, British, Australian, and New Zealand troops. During the period of truce, Canadian Red Cross workers were posted to Japan. Later, a few of us also went to Korea.

I was excited by the possibility of a new life of adventure and romance, and I assumed that because this was a United Nations operation that it was wise and just. Like most Canadians in Korea and Japan, I had little awareness of either the origins or the goals of the Korean War. I was proud to be part of Canadian history, but I was not yet aware of the wider implications—that we were intervening in a civil war and that the battle was really being waged by the US against communism.

Canadian historian Pierre Berton called Korea a "Yo-yo war." Others referred to it as police action. Canadian veterans, who received no official recognition after 40 years, called it "the forgotten war." By war's end, 200,000 South Koreans, 33,629 US soldiers, 3,360 UN allies (516 Canadians) and 1.5 million North Koreans and Chinese had been killed.

North Korea had invaded the South in June 1950. In 1951, Canada reluctantly agreed to send the 25th Canadian Brigade to Korea with instructions that their tour of duty would extend only to Korea. By the time Canada entered the war, the aim to unite the two Koreas was forgotten and it was all-out war against the communists. When the Chinese joined North Koreans to recapture Seoul, one and a half million refugees—mostly peasants whose rice fields had been destroyed—flooded south to Pusan.

By April 1951, outnumbered allied forces led by Canadians successfully held a hill at the Battle of Kapyong, ending the major fighting. The Canadians were awarded the US Distinguished Unit Citation for bravery. Over the next two years 1,000 meetings were held, but no peace agreement was reached. Meanwhile soldiers lived in deplorable conditions and many were killed on night patrols.

We Red Cross workers, civilians given the status of lieutenant, were part of the support services to Canada's brigade of rotating troops in Korea. We worked with Commonwealth forces as part of teams, which included Australian and British hospital workers. Most of us were trained social workers or Red Cross handicraft workers.

Brigadier Allard, the Commanding Officer of the Canadian Brigade, had requested Canadian Red Cross workers to work in leave centres in Japan (and later in Korea) as well as in British Commonwealth hospitals, which was the traditional Red Cross role. There was a suggestion that he had hoped the presence of our workers might help to reduce the high incidence of venereal disease in Canadian troops. However, I doubted that our nice Canadian centres would be much of an antidote to prostitution, (said to be) the number-one industry in postwar Japan.

Red Cross Work in Japan

Our job included visiting hospital wards with supplies, encouraging handicrafts projects, writing letters, and shopping, but mostly we spent time just talking to homesick patients. The rest of the time we spent at the Maple Leaf Club, a Canadian centre where homesick boys on R & R leave from Korea could drop in to read a hometown newspaper, enjoy Canadian beer, and talk to Red Cross girls from Canada. Although we heard many tales of bleak times in Korea and memories of home, we also heard many a tall tale as Aussies, Pommies and Canucks tried to outdo each other in competing for our attention.

At first I found it difficult to enter the Maple Leaf Club full of sex-starved soldiers who were watching and waiting to talk to the only Canadian girl on duty. Eventually I overcame my shyness and went up to talk to each of them, like a professional hostess. Some expected more, but we learned to avoid personal relationships and were well guarded by service personnel.

When we weren't working, we Red Cross workers lived in apartments in army quarters at Ebisu Camp in Tokyo and in Kure. We had our meals in the Officers' Mess, where traditional officers often resented this female presence. However, the OR (Other Rank) soldiers always seemed happy to see us and to talk about home.

Military life was strange and somewhat threatening at first—it took some adjusting to the protocol, authoritarianism, and other traditions with which I was unfamiliar. However, close friendships with other Red Cross workers soon helped me to overcome my initial anxiety. We had many laughs together and enjoyed exploring Japan.

I was fascinated with Japan—the smells and sounds and different foods and customs. I visited other parts of the country when I was on leave, including Nikko, Hiroshima, Kyoto and Miyajima. Japanese people were always helpful, but we made few personal friends. Postwar hardships endured.

After three weeks' orientation in Tokyo at the Maple Leaf Club, I was posted to Kure, on the Seto Inland Sea in western Japan, to work in the Britcom (British Commonwealth) General Hospital there. It was August, and the rainy season had given way to very hot, humid days, which are much worse than any Canada has to offer. Electric fans, lots of showers and salt tablets helped a bit. The poor hospital patients suffered the most, especially those in casts.

I liked the hospital work. It was a change from club work, but my feet got very sore. It was quite tiring working all day in the hospital and spending evenings and weekends shopping for the patients. Friday nights were also dance nights for Other Ranks, and we were expected to go regularly and jive madly in the sweltering heat. Our light-grey uniforms were soon dark with sweat. Fortunately I enjoy dancing.

One thing I didn't enjoy was learning about the double standard in army life. Although Red Cross women were usually treated with respect, I was appalled and disgusted on one occasion when two of us were told we were to go out with the Brigadier and the Colonel, who was the local Commanding Officer. We ended up in the bedrooms of a Japanese inn. I insisted on a taxi back to camp, feeling like I had been prostituted.

For the most part, though, I was having a wonderful time. One weekend while we were posted in Kure, my Red Cross friend Pam Whitehead and I spent a fascinating time at a Japanese hotel on the nearby island of Miyajima. We slept on the floor, were careful to remove our shoes at the proper times, wore kimonos, and ate hot, very hot, curried rice for breakfast—with chopsticks!

I was working in Kure during the prisoner-of-war exchange. Half of our Red Cross workers were in Korea and the rest of us met convoys as they arrived. Kure was the military headquarters in Japan for Commonwealth troops, so all the Aussie and British POWs were brought there from Korea. Except for those who were hospital cases, all the Canadian lads went directly to Tokyo. Patients in hospital were full of tales about patrols and skirmishes, and they anxiously waited to see if any of their buddies (or "cobbers," as the Aussies called them) would turn up. A large number of badly wounded soldiers arrived during the armistice time. It seemed worse somehow that they were shot during the last few days before the cease-fire. All were eager to get home and hoped they had a "homer," an injury bad enough to get them sent home. I wrote to my family, "I am beginning to realize that there is no justification for this war and am horrified by the senseless killing of young men."

Postings to Korea

Toward the end of November in 1953, I was posted for three months to Korea at the Canadian Field Services Station (like a MASH [Mobile Army Surgical Hospital] unit) and at Britcom General Hospital in Seoul. I flew over from Japan in an Australian army troop plane with string seats—a comfortable craft if you dressed warmly. En route to Seoul, I stopped off for a day at Pusan, Korea's point of entry. The city was as depressing as the troops had led us to believe, with dusty red soil and terrible living conditions for Koreans. They lived in shacks made of packing cases, with no floors, or at best, mud-walled huts with straw roofs. After an uneventful flight to Seoul, I hooked up with Red Cross pal Pam Whitehead and Barney Little, a Canadian paymaster whom I had known in Kure. I was driven to the Field Dressing Station by ambulance, over dusty roads through bleak, barren hills and grey countryside.

The weather was ferocious, with biting winter winds and freezing nights. Despite woollen underwear and sweaters layered under heavy battle dress topped with lined, windproof parkas, I was still cold, although getting used to it. I felt very sorry for the poor patients who were living in windy hospital huts with no uniforms, just pyjamas. We Red Cross girls lived together with the Canadian nursing Sisters in a Quonset hut with cement floors, covered windows, and no plumbing. I wrote home, "I have grown accustomed to the Korean climate. When one dresses for it, it is very exhilarating. I say this while sitting in a warm cozy mess—an hour ago in an unheated shower room, my feelings were quite different." Despite the cold, it was good to be back in a Canadian unit—back to coffee, less formality, beef instead of mutton, and the good old Canadian twang.

The work itself was much easier than it had been in Kure, with only four wards to service along with our duties at the Red Cross Centre, a large, frigid tent where patients came when they were able to be up. We girls had a challenging time working the kerosene lamps and stoves. One day I made the hour's drive to Seoul, twenty miles south, and went dancing at an American nightclub. Later we were invited to an American Artillery mess where we were royally entertained, presented with artillery scarves and pins, and served a wonderful feed.

It is easy to understand why we Red Cross girls loved our time in Korea. I, for one, was having such a good time! We women were so few in number that we were spoiled silly by house girls, drivers, and army personnel. As a result, I hated to return to Japan and so I was pleased to have another tour of duty in Korea. The men felt quite differently. They hated the country and the people, and counted the days and hours until they could either go home or go on leave to Japan. I hated their racist attitudes, and cringed when they called the Koreans "gooks."

The hospital where I worked in Seoul was a far cry from the tents and Quonset huts of the Advanced Dressing Station and the Field Dressing Station. However, it was hardly luxurious, especially the unheated tent that served as our Red Cross office. One thing that did impress me was a civilian hospital I visited, which was supported financially by the United Church of Canada. It was under the direction of a Canadian doctor and missionary who had been in Korea for 30 years. I was particularly impressed by the children's wards. There, little waifs convalesced in casts, or were aided in their recovery from bomb wounds or other ailments. I was also intrigued to see that the numerous amputees were being taught first how to make their own artificial limbs, and then how to use them. This was a new idea to most Koreans, who were accustomed to simply accepting disabilities, without trying to improve the situation.

Seoul showed evidence of much bombing and devastation. I wrote home, "Shacks are everywhere and the stench in back streets and alleys is unbelievable."

Christmas 1953, spent at the Canadian Field Dressing Station, was the one low point in my time in Korea. The day started at the new, unheated, unlit dining mess where we were told we were too late for breakfast. After distributing gifts to all patients at the station, I drove the 20 miles north to the Canadian Advance Dressing Station where there were no Red Cross girls—no girls at all, in fact. I spent the day visiting patients in tents, giving gifts, and talking to the soldiers. We thought of home and were a glum bunch indeed.

Spring of 1954 saw me back in Tokyo, at least temporarily. By this time I was feeling like a veteran myself, telling "warries" (war stories) with the best of them. Most of the Canadian units in Japan and Korea had changed. Soldiers that we knew so well were going home and new troops travelled directly to Korea. I wrote home, "The hardest part about this job is constantly saying goodbye."

In June of that year I was posted back to Korea, this time to Maple Leaf Park, the headquarters of the Canadian Brigade in North Korea, right at the front in the combat zone, where the Canadian Infantry Brigade remained as the advance unit during the truce. I lived with four other Red Cross workers in what I was now thinking of as a "comfortable" Quonset hut, and travelled by jeep each day to work at the new Canadian recreation centre established north of the 39th parallel. This centre was fairly well equipped, with a library, games room, writing rooms, and canteens. My job was to organize programs to help pass the time; they included tournaments, clubs, and even a square dance, despite the ratio of a few imported nurses and us Red Cross girls to 400 men. We also helped to keep up morale by taking turns announcing on the new Radio Maple Leaf, featuring musical requests from soldiers. My radio debut was not well received by the Australian "diggers" (soldiers), however, when I mistakenly called Melbourne the capital of Australia. Nonetheless, I continued doing my stint on the radio as long as I was there.

Despite diversions, war was never far away. Life in the combat zone was very restricted. We Red Cross girls couldn't go out by ourselves without drivers and escorts. From the recreation centre we looked across the hills at Chinese soldiers. The Demilitarized Zone, with hostile enemy soldiers facing each other, remains to this day.

For me personally, those fifteen months in Japan and Korea were a great time of adventure, romance, personal growth and the source of many, many nostalgic memories. During this historic period in my life I developed an international perspective and matured as a woman. I had many new experiences, made many friends, and in doing so I lost my shyness, gained confidence and a found delight in new adventures. I became comfortable with army life and related more easily to men, although I was still not looking for a permanent relationship. I had several romances with officers, but usually protected myself from serious relationships, knowing most were there for a short time and were usually married anyway. I gained a new vision of Canada through lads from all regions, and developed strong feelings about the Commonwealth.

I also developed a special enjoyment of Aussies—their carefree teasing and tall tales about life in Australia. Pam Whitehead, my Australian Red Cross pal, had become a close friend and she urged me to come to Australia after my tour in Japan was up. I felt I was destined to visit Australia, and Nevil Shute's book *A Town Like Alice* inspired me to see the Outback. It was not surprising that I would meet my future husband when leaving the land Down Under.

As valuable as my experiences in Asia may have been to my own personal growth, I left the Far East still wondering why the war in Korea was initiated, knowing nothing was won, and deploring the casualties and conditions for soldiers and civilians alike. Thirty-five years later, when I was an MP, I joined the Minister of Defence and Korean veterans on a pilgrimage to Japan and Korea. At the Demilitarized Zone, South Korean and US soldiers faced North Koreans in silent hostility, just as they had in 1954. Again I was sick at heart that peace was so unattainable.

CHAPTER 3

Following a Dream: Travels in the South Pacific

By the fall of 1954 I was ready for another new chapter in my life. I had finally decided to go to Australia before coming home. I finished my term in Japan and planned to travel by sea, stopping in Hong Kong. I had enough money for a return ticket to Canada but would have to work while in Australia.

On September 28, 1954, I sailed on the SS *Taiping,* a small, 80-passenger Australian semi-freighter bound for Sydney, Australia with a stopover in Hong Kong. From among the passengers we soon formed "our gang" comprised of David, a Kiwi captain I had known in Japan, Doug, an Australian fighter pilot, Lynn, another New Zealander, and myself. We organized our own fun on and off the ship.

Two days in colourful, colonial Hong Kong showed us the tragic disparity between hordes of refugees from China who were sleeping in the streets and minor British officials who were living in spacious apartments with servants. A typhoon forced us to put out to sea, where we were blown engineless toward the eye of the storm. Some passengers, fearing the end, sang "Nearer My God to Thee." I was more concerned with the Japanese war brides who were vomiting and in terror of the present danger. (Undoubtedly they were also concerned about the reception they would receive in Australia, where anti-Japanese sentiment was strong.)

In retaliation against the "white Australian policy" (which restricted

Asians from immigrating to Australia), we were refused landing in Indonesia. After several days of sailing on the gorgeous tropical seas where dolphins danced and the sunsets pierced my soul, we put in for a day in Cairns, Australia. The fresh pineapple tasted like ambrosia from the gods. We absorbed the lush tropical environment and toured the Great Barrier Reef.

On October 28 we disembarked in Sydney, where "our gang" surfed, partied and then sadly dispersed. I stayed in Sydney for a few days before sailing on a luxurious (and boring) ship down the east coast to Melbourne. There, Pam Whitehead and her family welcomed me and were wonderful hosts for several weeks. Pam, the Red Cross pal I had known in Korea, planned to come to Canada with me when I returned home.

Working in Melbourne

Since I had little cash, it was essential that I find work. After short-term jobs as a sales clerk and a playground supervisor, I joined Pam working for the Australian Red Cross at Heidelberg Veterans Hospital. The patients were delighted to have a Canuck to tease. They greeted me with, "Here comes Buckley's Canadiol with the lolly (candy) trolley." ("Buckley's Canadiol from blizzardly cold Canada" was a familiar cough remedy ad.) They confused me with nicknames for pounds, shillings, and pence which they called "quids, bobs, and tanners." I rarely balanced my books as a result.

In December I was a Canadian delegate to a World YWCA conference at Marysville, near Melbourne. Outstanding women from Asia, India, Thailand and the South Pacific, wearing colourful saris and sarongs, introduced me to a new international perspective. For Christmas the Whiteheads took Pam and me camping in South Australia, where desert winds brought 109-degree heat and unbearable flies provided a strange contrast to the previous year's cold and lonely Christmas in Korea.

Meanwhile, my plans to visit Australia's Outback were taking shape. I would be joined on my travels by Jacqueline Robitaille (now Van Campen) from Quebec, and her friend Claire, another French Canadian from Winnipeg. Jackie and I had met first in late 1953 when we were both Canadian Red Cross workers attached to Commonwealth Forces in Japan. She was naive and full of fun. When she first came to Japan, she spoke little English, and the soldiers took great delight in teaching her their version.

When Jackie and I were posted together in North Korea to work at the Army Recreation Centre at brigade headquarters there we became close friends. She and I were both fascinated by Aussies and with continuing our travels among them. And we were both fans of Nevil Shute's book *A Town Like Alice*, the inspiration for our shared obsession with visiting Alice Springs. Jackie agreed to meet me in Melbourne when her tour of duty ended, and, along with Claire, together we would explore the Outback.

The three of us shared a cheap room in Melbourne and started to plan our hitchhiking adventure. We ate sparingly, saved every "bob," and enjoyed sharing our different Canadian cultures. Our youth hostel mates helped us to make a pup tent with collapsible poles. We bought a tiny 'chuffer' stove, a first-aid kit, and second-hand packs and sleeping bags. My sleeping bag was light, so we decided I should sleep sandwiched between Jackie and Claire. (This would require all three of us to turn together several times a night.) We would carry a two-day supply of dehydrated staples, and we would hitchhike where we could. Our ultimate goal was Alice Springs, close to 2,000 kilometres away. I was keen for the adventure and fun and perhaps hardships that we would experience. I wanted to learn all I could about Australia and Australians.

Travel in the Outback

The following are highlights from the diary I kept during this period.

Melbourne, April 6, 1955
An alarm pierced the cold damp dreariness of the winter morning. We dashed from the dingy room we had called home, doubled up by packs and laughter, ready to test our hitchhiking skills. The second driver who picked us up was a madman. He drove like a maniac, honking, but never stopping, at intersections. The inevitable finally happened when a lady driver refused to give him her right of way. A side-on crash ensued and we all landed in a police station with we three as witnesses. Our friend declared belligerently that his father was on the London police force and he knew his rights. The officer

(probably thinking "bloody Pommie bastard") settled the matter with a summons signed by the victim's husband, who happened to be the local chief of police. We escaped.

The next day, after travelling the Ninety Mile Desert, we were picked up by a young couple who covered us with a tarp in the back of their truck. Choked with dust, Jackie complained that her "hairs" needed cutting. Claire obliged and an interesting brush cut was born. More moans from Jackie!

In Adelaide we saw koala bears, fed wallabies, saw emus, a camel, and kookaburras. In Quorn, a lively frontier town, we were feeling devilish, so we went into a local lounge for a beer (women were not allowed in the bar). We had been told that Aussie men have three loves: beer, races, and women—in that order.

The Ghan train to Alice Springs was an adventure in itself. Other passengers joined us on the back platform. A bewhiskered old 'swaggie' with his swag (rolled blankets) and his billy can for tea told us tall stories of his adventures until the conductor made him join "the blacks" (aborigines) in the rear car. We passed miles of desolate red desert dotted with sagebrush and the occasional water bore. The flies and the heat were both intolerable. Eventually we arrived in Alice Springs, a pretty town and oasis in the desert.

Policemen had advised us along our earlier journey, and in "Alice" they hosted us. We camped near the bachelor's quarters, enjoying hot water and a breakfast of goanna [monitor lizard] meat roasted underground by aboriginal trackers. "Good tucker," they said. And it was.

Policemen told us tales of aborigines, showed us boomerangs of the Arunta tribe (which do not return), and demonstrated how to use a 'woomera,' which holds a spear. They took us to visit a Catholic Mission, a flying doctor base that connects Outback families, providing schooling and medical services by radio. We enjoyed a cattle roundup and Australian-rules football—much better than our "sissy" grid-iron football, we were told.

By mid-April it was time to leave Alice Springs. The police arranged a lift for us on a transport truck to Tenants Creek. Peter, our driver, stopped frequently to check his failing brakes but failed to stop *when I had an urgent call from nature. (Hanging from a twenty-foot-high transport truck is quite an experience.) Eventually Peter dumped us in total darkness at a remote water bore where we were fearful of snakes and roving drunken visitors. Next day a driver came early and we joined aborigines on the back of the truck. One woman was very interested in my high-style green raincoat, and it disappeared when she did. I imagined how this haute couture item entertained her tribe in the rainless desert.*

In Queensland we hit tropical rains. We shared a caravan with a family of four while waiting for the water in flooded creeks to recede. After a few days in Cairns we headed to Sydney. Hitchhiking was very difficult here and we had long waits. Our most memorable and miserable ride was on the back of a transport truck, this time carrying cow-hides. It took many hours to rid ourselves of the stench.

Farewell to Australia

When we finally arrived in Sydney we had to part, sadly. Jackie and Claire were continuing their travels through Asia to India and Europe. I was leaving for a six-week working holiday in New Zealand. Ultimately I would connect with Aussie friend Pam to return to Canada by ship. As Jackie, Claire and I went our separate ways, we took with us many memories of many friendly people and a great adventure to "the Alice."

Why was I so fascinated by Australia and Australians? It started in Japan with the teasing and the broad accents of "digger" soldiers who told us many tales of their homeland. My Australian friend, Pam Whitehead, whom I knew in Korea, had welcomed me into her family and she accompanied me back to Canada. The country, particularly the Outback, was an intriguing contrast to Canada, as was aboriginal life. I was so hooked on Australia and Aussies when I left in June 1955 that an Aussie husband was predictable.

Some say you can't go back, and in the case of Alice Springs they were right. When I returned on a visit in 2000, I was extremely disappointed to find a sophisticated tourist town in place of the simpler Outback centre I remembered.

New Zealand, Fiji and Home

When I first arrived in New Zealand I was staying at the "Y" in Christchurch. David Doake, whom I knew in Tokyo and on the *Taiping,* was teaching in Christchurch and suggested this would be a good central place from which to see the South Island while working. He and his family made me feel right at home.

I found New Zealanders to be much like Australians—more conservative and English, perhaps because they are fairly isolated. There and in 'Aussie,' living standards were fairly high (no central heating!) and there were more jobs than there were workers to fill them. This seemed to make everyone a bit complacent and easy-going. People were very sports minded, with football, soccer, swimming, tennis, horse racing, trots, dog races, and cricket all being popular. Everyone participated, either by playing or betting. Beer-drinking in pubs for men and playing the lotteries were also national occupations here, as they were in Aussie. Locals were scornful of TV, which had not yet arrived in New Zealand.

I finally found a job waitressing in a fancy restaurant. People were very friendly and customers tipped occasionally (one couple gave me a lovely greenstone ring). It stayed cold, and people wore coats in the restaurant. I was now living with an elderly woman whose family wanted her to have company in exchange for a room.

In July I spent a week travelling around New Zealand. Although I enjoyed it, the trip was not as much fun as previous trips with friends. Women I had met at the World YWCA Conference in Australia entertained me in Wellington and Hamilton. I even had breakfast in bed. Such a novelty after being a waitress and domestic in Christchurch!

On the bus going north we passed cattle and sheep farms, and saw reforested pine trees, Australian gums, many flowering trees, scotch thistle, and yellow wattle. We saw rabbits, wild pigs, swans, tui birds, fantail birds, deer, and coloured fish. When we arrived in the North Island it was snowing in Rotorua, home of fascinating thermal activity and Maori people. I wandered alone along steaming paths with occasional geysers and came upon men cooking a wild pig in a thermal pool. They showed me how food was cooked underground by thermal pressure, and explained that steam is also used for central heating, hothouses, and electricity.

Not long after that I said goodbye to New Zealand. On July 20, 1955, I met my friend Pam Whitehead in Auckland where we boarded the SS *Oronsay*, a large Pacific & Orient liner with capacity for hundreds of passengers. We were in second class, where all the fun was. Pam and I shared a cabin, and we made some good friends on board ship. Robbie, an artist from Glasgow, sketched us all. Claude Mitchell was a loud Aussie and a great tease. Two younger Aussie guys planned to buy a car in Vancouver to travel across Canada. We played games and joined the shenanigans as we crossed the equator, where the water is supposed to reverse its direction of flow going down the sink.

This was the first time I met Claude, who years later was to become my husband. He was about forty, and with his clipped mustache he looked a bit like David Niven. His loud, bass, Aussie voice dominated the deck. I thought him a brash show-off who loved to shock people with his macho attitudes and sexist jokes. He hung out with several Aussie girls and I spent time with Robbie, Pam, and other friends. I never expected to see him again after we disembarked.

We arrived in Suva, the capital of Fiji, several days after leaving Auckland. On board ship we had made friends with a Fijian girl, Connie, who had been living in New Zealand for some years. With persuasion, she had brought out her ukulele and we had sung songs well into the night. Connie had told us that Suva was a filthy city filled with "dirty Indians," whom she obviously hated. We learned that in recent years there had been such an influx of Indians to Fiji that they now outnumbered Fijians, and moreover, had taken over most trading and commercial interests. There was little mixing between the races and even less intermarriage. There were also many Chinese in Fiji and a minority of whites, although Fiji was a British colony controlled by the British government.

We were greeted on arrival by crowds of Fijians and Indians. The welcoming Fijian band and policemen were most impressive. The policemen were huge chaps with bushy, afro-style hair, and were dressed in short, tight wrap-around white skirts trimmed with red stripes, topped off with black, brass-buttoned jackets.

Pam and I had decided to roam around on our own rather than go on an organized tour. We invited Nancy, a Chinese girl, to join us. At one point, we took a picture of a group of kids—a Fijian boy minding his baby brother and playing with an Indian boy who was also minding a baby. At least the kids seemed to be oblivious to racial differences. We also went to the Fijian market. An elderly Fijian man who was sitting under a coconut tree showed us how he braided palm leaves together into baskets and hats. He gathered coral from the local reefs, dyed it, and then sold it in the palm-leaf baskets. Generally, though, the Fijians seemed to take a complacent approach to life. They stacked their sleeping babies away under the counters and sat on the floor chatting and eating. Occasionally they made an effort to sell to the tourists—"real cheap bargain." When Nancy treated us to a Chinese meal, the Chinese customers watched Pam and me nonchalantly wielding chopsticks.

After a short bus trip outside the capital city, we left Suva to a wonderful send-off. The dock was crowded with people of many races in different costumes. The band played, our ship's horn tooted, the smokestack sprayed us all with soot, and we set sail. As a farewell for many kindnesses, the ship sent up parachuted rockets and fireworks in *au revoir*. I left feeling that I was more aware of the many diverse races I had encountered—aborigines, Melanesians, Polynesians—and of the impact of colonialism, which still exists today.

Our last stop on our South Pacific journey was the island of Oahu, in Hawaii. On August 1st we stopped at Honolulu for a day, enjoying an island tour with the "First Class" Hawaiian American friends I had met on the ship, a surfing experience on an outrigger surfboard, and a wonderful dinner party. We left enjoying the scent of many leis around our necks—gifts from our friends. The leis floated back to shore, showing we would return. For now it was time to go home.

CHAPTER 4

Romance in Vancouver and Vienna

Our homecoming to Canada was a joyful one. I was delighted that Aunt Hilda Dutton came west to meet Pam and me in Vancouver. Her Canadian accent seemed strange to my Aussie-tuned ears. After a visit with her, Pam and I set out on our journey across the country to Ontario, sharing the costs of a car rented by two of our Aussie shipmates. We slept in the car (I tooted the horn as I turned over) while they tented.

There was great excitement when we arrived in Cayuga, as preparations were underway for my sister Betty's marriage to Jack Speers. I hardly had a chance to show my thousands of slides to anyone! I was a bridesmaid while Pam was the official flower girl. It was great to be home with family and friends.

Settling in Vancouver—A Stormy Romance

In the fall of 1955, after Betty's wedding and after Pam had settled in Toronto, I flew to Vancouver to begin work as Program Director at Alexandra Neighbourhood House. I shared a waterfront apartment with Cleta Herman, a social work friend. Later we moved to a large, old house on Point Grey Road with Dorothy Hunt. Our house became a hangout for pals and for parties. A tiny extra bedroom was used rent-free by rotating male friends who were supposed to keep the wood furnace burning.

It was wonderful to be home, but soon life in Vancouver took on a certain routine. For a little excitement that winter, Dorothy and I took the *Sun* newspaper's free skiing lessons on Grouse Mountain. By spring we thought we were trained, and we booked a ski holiday in Banff. We soon lost confidence and almost our lives when we skied (mostly on hands and knees) down what we thought was a lonely mountain run. I was horrified when we reached the bottom and were told that this was not a run, but a very dangerous avalanche area. That put an end to my skiing adventures.

Then, a few weeks later, Claude Mitchell, the Australian whom I had met on the *Oronsay,* arrived at Cleta's door, and another kind of adventure began. Claude had decided to look me up after seeing me on a TV show called "Almanac," where I was interviewed about my adventures in the Australian Outback. The interviewer and I, in jeans, sat on a log outside a pup tent from which a continuous line of men exited (they re-entered off camera)—giving me a rather questionable reputation.

On the ship Claude had seemed a boisterous show-off with a loud voice and a raunchy sense of humour who was friendly with everyone. Now he was living in Vancouver with his brother Des, working in cable TV, and planning to take this new technology back to Australia. I had not been a special friend of Claude's, but was pleased to see a former shipmate.

Claude soon became a regular drop-in at Cleta's apartment, and he frequently invited us both on excursions—camping, boomerang throwing, and cooking steak over a campfire. He introduced me to his family, including brother Des and his wife Ann, their daughters Patti-Ann and Jennifer, and their three-year-old, redheaded son "Bluey" (Billy), whom we often took with us on drives.

I put up with Claude's nonsense and enjoyed our outings. However, I was irritated when Claude came unannounced to visit me at work, and was embarrassed by his antics at parties where most of my friends were social workers. He loved to shock them with outrageous remarks and used to say, "All social workers come out from under rocks." They were not amused. I am sure they wondered why I was "going with" Claude, and I was often upset by his blunt Aussie behaviour. Of course his sexist behaviour became more pronounced in the presence of especially prim people.

There were other sources of tension between us, too. Claude and I came from very different backgrounds. He grew up in Melbourne in a working-class family during the Depression. After leaving school at 14 and a blow-up at home, he went roaming for a year, living often near starvation. Eventually he worked in Sydney in the radio industry. During the war he built radar stations in New Guinea. When he returned to Australia, he bought his own radio shop. He had always loved the circus, and some years later he sold his business, built a "carousel" (merry-go-round), and joined a circus travelling north to Cairns during the winter months.

I, on the other hand, had grown up in small-town Ontario in a supportive family of professionals with whom I had but minor skirmishes. I stayed in school and went on to complete a master's degree, working along the way, before paying off my debts by applying my social work degree to work in Canada, then abroad.

Although my middle-class conformity was often upset by Claude's loud behaviour and his delight in shocking people, there was a lot about him that I liked. I admired his independence, his versatility (he could fix anything), his intelligence, and his sense of fun. He was largely self-educated and extremely well read. He loved languages and was a champion of the Australian idiom. He hated injustice, always helped the underdog, and once ran as a candidate for the Australian Labour Party.

Despite our differences, Claude was persistent and gradually overcame my resistance to a relationship. We had a common interest in people, in social justice, and in travel, and we had fun together. Claude was sensitive to my inhibitions and we moved slowly into a relationship, which for me was an awakening.

Unfortunately, Claude and his brother had a business failure and Claude lost his savings. Our relationship was at a standstill, and Claude decided to take a trip to Mexico to let me think things over. He stayed instead with a friend in Hollywood, doing odd jobs. Although I missed him, I decided we were unsuited. In December 1956, I accepted a Red Cross job in Vienna, working with Hungarian refugees. Our romance was delayed by world events.

Vienna—Working with Hungarian Refugees

When I was recruited on short notice by the Red Cross for work in Vienna, I became part of an effort by the League of Red Cross Societies to provide relief camps across Austria. People in Hungary, who had lived under Russian occupation during the Second World War and were now part of the Soviet Union, were unhappy with their living conditions and the communist regime. When the revolution of 1956 collapsed, people left the country in droves. At one point, 6,000 people a day were seeking asylum in tiny, war-torn Austria, where over 100,000 refugees were already living in permanent camps. The Canadian Red Cross was to operate two of the new camps set up by the League, providing personnel and supplies.

I arrived in Vienna with members of our Canadian Red Cross team in December 1956. Our diverse group was to work in Brigittaspital Camp. Dan, a social worker, was our team leader. Paul, a Hungarian Canadian who spoke English and German as well as Hungarian, had run a restaurant in Toronto and was our food expert. Ina was a nurse with years of experience in northern Saskatchewan. Marian, who had worked for Eaton's, was in charge of refugee clothing and stores. I was seconded from Alexandra Neighbourhood House to be a recreation worker. We later hired an Austrian doctor who spoke only German, and a charming Austrian secretary who also spoke English. We were keen to do a good job and soon bonded as a family. I was excited to be on a new adventure and concerned for the plight of the refugees. Letters to my family at home recall a time of great upheaval and personal development.

On January 7, 1957, I wrote from Vienna:

Before starting work in Brigittaspital Refugee Camp, we celebrated New Year's Eve in true Viennese fashion—wining, dining, singing, and toasting everyone in a tavern restaurant in the basement of an old monastery. After midnight we joined others in the streets. It seemed all Vienna was celebrating in the snow, although the customary dancing in the streets was curtailed in sympathy for the suffering in Hungary.

On January 1st, reality descended. Brigittaspital Camp is in a former maternity hospital—once the pride of Vienna but now almost destroyed by our wartime bombs and by the Russians who occupied this zone until last year. They had ripped out all fixtures and even took doors and windows when they left. Our future basement kitchen has no walls, so meals are catered in dormitories temporarily. Not appetizing, those refugee meals.

The building was bad enough but then we saw the living conditions of Hungarian refugees—sleeping on straw mats on the floor with no privacy, no hot water, no place to sit or eat except on those mats, with nothing to do except line up in long cues at emigration offices. We soon learned that after twelve years of deprivation, these were minor hardships since they hoped to leave soon for a new life. I was worried about kids playing in the bomb debris until I was reminded they had survived being tranquillized to cross a very dangerous border and this was fun. I began to realize that in Canada we live a very naive and sheltered life.

I spent the first week visiting people in their dormitories, trying to get to know their needs and helping other teammates with basic necessities. We obtained beds and mattresses, started a cleaning campaign, and ordered supplies. It seemed ridiculous to try to organize recreation when there was no space to use and I had no idea what people needed and wanted. However by the second week, we arranged to use the temporary kitchen as a meeting room, despite no heat and the smell of food. I found a number of Hungarians who speak English (most younger people speak Russian and German), and they have begun to help us as interpreters.

People have told me the children needed a program first—for their own sake and to give their parents some peace. Toys were donated and we've started supervised play periods. We discovered several teachers who helped to set up a school. (I was told later that one teacher was also the camp prostitute. She was alone and I suspect had no funds.) Parents want English taught first, then geography about the countries the children will be going to, then arithmetic and handicrafts.

We were lucky to find a young man who is a physical education specialist. He has developed a wonderful gym program for children ages 3 to 12 with no equipment except a few mattresses. He is training others to take over when he leaves (a constant problem). The kids were a joy to watch, and parents came in to watch the fun.

This week we started English lessons for adults. They use the smelly kitchen (now heated) for a lounge with games, radio, and films once a week. Hungarian poetry performances are most dramatic. A dance is planned for next Sunday. Next week we are going to form a camp council with elected representatives from each room to help run the camp. We hope to have sewing machines and a workshop soon.

The teenagers badly need something to do, and gang problems are beginning. With the help of a Hungarian student who lives nearby and who volunteers each day, we have started a youth club. They meet afternoons, have English and geography classes, help with work projects, and are beginning to plan social events.

In Vancouver we talked about generic social work. Now I know what it is—giving out soap, trying to organize programs, and running up four cold flights of stairs for every bit of equipment. I am also the welfare officer. This means trying to help people to find lost relatives, helping people who have immigration problems, or who are depressed and need activities. I find it heartbreaking not to be able to speak the language when people need help so much, but I manage with the use of interpreters.

Many hilarious things happen each day which help to ease tensions. Five of us are crowded into one office along with six to eight Hungarians and Austrians and two or three interpreters. I find myself using sign language with fellow Canadians. We break into hysterical laughter at the confusion—and refugees join in.

After hours we try to forget camp life and enjoy Vienna. At present we live in a comfortable downtown hotel (feeling guilty) since all local hotels are crowded with refugees. Dinner at night is a ritual since Paul, who knew Vienna before 1948, feels it is his duty to take us to a different place each night—always with wine, Viennese or Hungarian food, and either a zither playing "The Third Man Theme" or a haunting gypsy band. We have been to the ballet and plan to go to the opera in the glorious old Vienna Opera House, which has been restored.

Paul is one of the livelier members of the team, and when he invited me to go to the famous Hunters' Ball, I was quite flattered, even though I was somewhat ambivalent given my relationship with

Claude. Some of the Red Cross people from other camps were there, too.

It was a wonderful experience. Vienna was at its peak. Everyone who could afford it was involved. There were huge ballrooms and orchestras in each room, with everyone dressed up in peasant clothes and their hunters' suits. Paul, being very orthodox and from Vienna, wanted me to rent a dress, but I didn't want to do that. I wore a dress I have that is very much like a peasant dress, so I fit in okay. We swooped around to the Viennese waltzes through the various rooms. It was beautiful.

Circumstances in Austria as a whole were not nearly so glamorous. I found the Austrians to be relaxed, friendly people, but I wondered how they could continue to take in millions of refugees when their own people were poor and unemployed, and thousands of people displaced by World War II were still living in camps around the country. Emigration was at a standstill, and many people could be facing permanent refugee status, but large numbers of Hungarians were still streaming across the Austrian border via Yugoslavia. An Austrian doctor told me, "Austria simply can't support it on her economy and small size. Yet she can't afford not to take these people."

One bitterly cold Sunday in mid-January we five Canadians left Vienna for the Hungarian border. Our Hungarian driver, Paul, a former car racer, whisked us past tiny villages which looked like something out of a European movie with their rows of attached cottages made of painted brick. Peasants dressed in knickers with long jackets and tams socialized on the streets.

We finally reached the town of Anchow, near the Hungarian border, where Austria reaches into Hungary in a long peninsula. Refugees crossed into Austria at many different points along the border: some came through the forests, others swam the canal or waded through icy swamplands. They usually travelled by night and in small parties, led by guides who repeated the journey many times.

After they reached Austria, refugees were housed temporarily in Anchow's Red Cross Centre, and then moved on to our camps further in Austria until they were able to migrate. When we arrived at the Centre, the Austrian and German Red Cross people gave us a warm welcome, serving us hot chocolate and then tea with rum, and showing us the fruit and chocolate bars they were giving to refugees. (You can imagine what this symbolized to people who had not seen such luxuries for 15 years.)

It was dusk as we drove along a muddy, potholed road toward Hungary. There were no houses on the bleak muddy fields, and we saw no signs of life beyond a lone crow and a rabbit until we saw a man trudging slowly through the mud—a black speck on the gloomy horizon. The middle-aged peasant was dressed in a lightweight coat, no gloves, carrying a pair of shoes. He explained that he had been guiding refugees across the border to Austria. Although some Hungarian police along the border were sympathetic, he said, one never knew when secret police would be among them. Refugee parties crossed wherever the grapevine said the sympathetic police might be posted.

The man accepted our offer of a ride, and we crawled along slowly over the bumpy road until the border tower and flag came into view. We stopped to let our man take cover in the woods, but he decided to take a chance and cross in the open. As we approached the canal on foot, we could see the Hungarian police on the opposite shore and hear shots in the distance. We recognized several men in the Hungarian police uniform (we later learned we were on Hungarian soil). Although we were well protected by Red Cross insignia, we feared for our friend. However, in a relaxed, nonchalant way he explained to the police that he had left a week ago but now wanted to return home. The police questioned him and took him away and we gathered he had convinced them. All the way back we wondered how this man and the many refugees travelling on foot would make out that night.

Second Thoughts—Claude Arrives

When I left Vancouver for Vienna, I had convinced myself that my relationship with Claude had no future. However, I had not been entirely honest with myself. As soon as we separated in Vancouver I was overcome with loneliness and longing for him. He had been very upset when I phoned him in Los Angeles to tell him that I had accepted a six-month job with the Canadian Red Cross, working in a Hungarian refugee camp. He didn't want me to go.

Claude wrote to me every day while I was away, pouring out his love and longing, and urging me to express my own repressed feelings. To begin with, my letters to him were quite impersonal, but Claude insisted that I tell him how I felt. I finally told him how much his decision to leave me to "think things over" had hurt and upset me, and that I had wept in the car for hours. "How sweet and loving you are and how considerate— and how warm and comfortable it was when we were together," I wrote. "We enjoyed so many good times, especially when we were alone." He liked this letter.

I longed for Claude's letters each day and often broke down when I read them—a new reaction for stalwart, cool Margaret. Claude quoted sections from Kahlil Gibran's *The Prophet*. "Think not that you can direct the course of love, for love if it finds you worthy directs your course." Both of us were feeling depressed, and I was tired from working seven-day weeks. Fortunately my teammates were very supportive.

Claude was concerned for my safety in the refugee camp, and I was upset when he criticized the refugees for keeping us apart. When I chastised him for his attitude, he was contrite, acknowledging that it wasn't the refugees' fault that we missed each other terribly. Claude also commented on the Middle East war and phoned the Israeli Consulate to indicate his support for Israel. I survived a revolution at the camp and enjoyed the opera in the beautifully renovated Vienna Opera House. We were literally miles apart.

That distance allowed me to realize that I loved Claude and wanted to be with him. His devotion and persistence broke my lifetime pattern of repressing my feelings, allowing me to respond to his love. I still had some concerns about the future, since he had no job, but Claude dismissed this worry, saying that our being together must come first and that he would recognize opportunities when they came. I realized that I was conditioned by the attitude of professionals who put a job and security first, while Claude had no such reservations and was confident that our love was based on more than "security" and that we would face the future together.

Eventually I wrote to Claude, suggesting that we be married as soon as possible, and he was overjoyed. Although I still had some reservations, I put these aside. I thought that this was our destiny and that love would overcome all. Nonetheless, I did write to Claude with some of my concerns, and he responded. "I did not realize I was such an uncouth colonial until I read a list of my faults. You ask if I think you are a prude. Well I do think you are, but it does not alter my love for you. For your sake I will make more effort to be more Canadian and less Australian."

Later Claude wrote, "We will have a great life to live together with understanding, tolerance, a sense of humour, idealism, concern for our fellow man, music, work, discussion, a future to build together, our house that I want to build with your help. We will have children. We both love children so very much." I was very moved, and when I wrote back, added to his list: "friends we both love, a love of nature and all things beautiful."

By this time Claude was almost broke and working for free in Los Angeles, but after several weeks of loneliness he was determined to get to Toronto, and then, somehow, to Vienna to join me. He began a cross-country bus trip to Toronto, where he stayed with my Aunt Alma. He visited with my family, and phoned me in Vienna. We were both very emotional. Despite the antagonism of Albert Batten, the senior Red Cross officer in Austria, Claude arrived in Vienna on March 14, 1957.

A Wedding in Vienna

I waited at the Vienna airport for Claude to arrive. We had been separated for four months. I cherished his daily love letters, realizing how much I missed him. We had finally agreed by letter that Claude should come to join me in Vienna, help as a volunteer in the refugee camp, and the two of us could decide on our future.

My female teammates were encouraging our romance and Marian had a job waiting for Claude. We had thought we could get permission for him to come on a Red Cross flight. However, the higher-ups in Canada refused him. He was stuck in Toronto, almost broke, and wondering what to do next. Then my wonderful Aunt Alma, with whom Claude was staying, loaned him money to buy a ticket so we could be reunited. But as I waited, I wondered if old differences that had separated us would reappear.

Finally he arrived—grinning from ear to ear and chewing gum. I was enveloped in a big bear hug. "How the hell are you, Luv?" his deep

Australian voice boomed out. My heart sang. I was overjoyed that he was in Vienna, and introduced him to my wonderful, supportive colleagues.

Claude moved into a cheap room near our hotel and he used our showers. I was happy that we were together again, and although I was still embarrassed at times by Claude's exhibitionism, my teammates soon accepted Claude and made him part of our group.

The refugees and staff were excited at the prospect of a wedding. Tony, the chef, promised to make a glorious Austrian wedding cake. Anna presented me with a Hungarian doll, and Hilda made a heart-shaped cushion (which I still have) that declares, "My heart sends it to you warmly." All seven members of the Red Cross team wanted to perform at the wedding, so we planned to be married twice: in a German civil ceremony and in an English church wedding—which ultimately became a double ceremony.

Other arrangements were more complicated. The bureaucrats of Vienna had a heyday trying to sort out why an Australian citizen was marrying a Canadian citizen who was working in a Hungarian refugee camp in Vienna. "They sent me to five different places and stamped everything except my backside," Claude said in frustration.

The elderly English minister we located was overjoyed to officiate again. He performed a long High Anglican service, complete with an ancient stole which he wrapped around our hands for the double ceremony. Claude later told friends, "There I was, a bloody atheist, tied up in church while the old boy reminisced about his time in India. We were a captive audience."

After the celebrations we left by train for Dürnstein, a medieval town in Austria where Richard the Lionhearted was held prisoner during the Crusades. It was dark when we arrived. Exhausted, we stumbled along the winding cobblestone road carrying a heavy suitcase. An old man directed us to the inn, where we hoped for a lovely room overlooking the Danube. Claude had phoned ahead and was told there was a vacancy.

When we got to the inn we were treated with suspicion. There was no reservation, they said, and as this was a busy weekend they were full up. We pleaded with them, but to no avail. Finally they cleared out a tiny room for us. And so we weary honeymooners spent our wedding night on a cot in the linen closet, wondering what adventures tomorrow would bring.

Motorcycling in Europe

In May 1957 we left Vienna and the refugee camp on a noisy 30-year-old Ariel motorcycle which Claude loved to repair with beer bottle caps and fencing wire. I travelled in luxury in the classy "bi-wagon" (side car), which had room in the nose for a two-litre Chianti bottle, which was refilled periodically with *vin du pays* (the local wine). For snacks we used the pâté de fois gras and other donated delicacies not suitable for camp use, which had been given to us by the camp chef. Our few clothes and wedding presents were tucked around me.

We headed for the Tyrol in western Austria. As we climbed the Alps we hit a blinding blizzard. Claude put on his Snoopy-style leather helmet with ear-flaps but was soon covered in snow while I was snug in the covered side car. When we were forced to stop in a deserted area, an old man invited us into his cabin to have tea and to warm up. Claude practised his German.

Eventually we made it to Salzburg, where Claude had booked us into the "Natur Freund Haus," which turned out to be a nudist camp. We stayed, clothed. We loved the narrow winding streets where Mozart had lived and enjoyed a marionette opera. We moved on to Munich and eventually to Innsbruck. There we loaded the motorcycle on a flatcar and took the train across Austria to Italy.

Border crossing caused considerable confusion as we had an Australian passport, a Canadian passport, and a British motorcycle with an Austrian license plate. When we clipped a passing car and Claude tried to placate the driver in his struggling Italian, a wise German waved us on, saying *"Auf Wiedersehen."*

In Venice, Claude's hidden romantic streak blossomed and we splurged and travelled the canals in a gondola. We drove through lovely Italian hills to Florence, found a place to stay in a cheap *pension,* and enjoyed the marvellous art and architecture despite their wartime damage. Michelangelo's "David" has remained in my soul. Anyone who has witnessed the perfection and awesome size of this work will understand how intensely it can affect a person.

The motorcycle and our backsides needed a rest, so we took a train to Rome to be tourists. Some days later we left Italy on the motorcycle, checking out the Leaning Tower of Pisa en route. A lovely ride along the Mediterranean and the French Riviera ended with a dramatic visit to Monaco's elegant Monte Carlo Casino. The full blast of our ancient motorcycle reverberated against lavish buildings as we drove up the curved driveway. When we arrived at the door of the Casino in our refugee clothes, the gendarmerie quickly escorted us out.

In Barcelona we stayed with a family in a B & B. Our hostess was a marvellous cook who served meals at 11 p.m., including a delicious pigeon Claude had caught on the roof. The jovial host took us to a nightclub to see flamenco dancing, and to a gory bullfight. Claude loved the bullfight tradition. Both men praised me because I didn't throw up like several women around us.

We were reluctant to leave sunny Spain, but after several days we headed north to France. Claude usually looked for cheap *pensions* outside the larger towns. He found one late one night. We woke up in the middle of the night feeling cold and damp. Water was seeping through floor tiles and the mattress was damp. We put on rain gear and crawled back into bed but it was no use. At dawn we left. The sun came up as we rode off through red poppy fields of southern France. When we stopped to enjoy the scenery I prepared pâté on biscuits and a large Chianti to warm us. Claude returned from the woods with a bouquet of poppies. He then entertained me by doing a "flying angel"— driving the motorcycle one handed, with a leg and arm extended. I sang in accompaniment.

I did not enjoy Paris very much. I was not feeling well, the Parisians seemed unfriendly, and prices were high. However, we did the tourist things: visited the Eiffel Tower, the Louvre, artists along the Seine, and took in a tour of nightclubs. It seemed time to move on.

Just where to move on to now that my refigee job was over was the question. The possibilities seemed to be South Africa, where Claude had a job offer, Toronto, or Australia, and, since I was on leave and had a job to return to, the West Coast of Canada. By the time we reached London we had decided we would settle in Vancouver.

In London we stayed in a boarding house in cockney Clapham Common and from there began to absorb the great city—the Tower, the British Museum, the pubs, and the music halls. Claude was fascinated with sailing and we went up the Thames to see Sir Francis Chichester's famous boat in which he had sailed around the world solo. When we stopped to watch Prince Philip play polo, Claude stole one of Philip's "balls"—a cherished souvenir. It entered his repertoire of jokes thereafter.

Claude finally let his beloved motorcycle go for $1.00 to a traveller heading back to Europe. (This was essential because it was registered in Austria and could not remain in England.) We booked on an eight-passenger freighter headed over the North Atlantic to Quebec and boarded her in Ireland. The rough seas made me seasick for most of the trip.

After we landed we headed for Cayuga. My stepmother, Helen, had a Cayuga reception for us and even persuaded Claude to cut the grass (with the help of a beer from Dad, which Helen had opposed). Dad had married Helen after Betty left home. She had been a respected, shy English teacher for each of us in high school. She blossomed as she adapted to us, her new family, and we grew to love her.

After a visit with my family, we headed west. We stopped in Edmonton to see my new niece Jane, Betty and Jack's darling baby. Finally we arrived in Vancouver and realized it was the most beautiful place of our travels. We were home!

My time in Austria, and later, Claude's and my honeymoon trip around Europe were turning points in my life. I gained valuable experience working in a refugee camp, which led to future work in community development. When Claude arrived in Vienna and we were married, a whole new life had opened up for me

CHAPTER 5

A Life Crisis, Family, Travel

Claude and I came home to Vancouver in the spring of 1957, when the bulbs and rhododendrons were blooming. We rented an apartment in Kitsilano and began to settle into our life together in Canada. We had no idea that our lives were about to change dramatically.

I returned to work at Alexandra Neighbourhood House and Claude began to search for work. Since he had limited Canadian experience or contacts, it was difficult for him. For a time he tried to sell mutual funds for the company his brother Des had founded, but he was not a natural salesman of abstract investments and refused to "bullshit" the customers.

Although in some ways these were uncertain times, Claude and I were certain about one thing: we both wanted children. I hadn't had a "physical" since the summer before, when I had visited my doctor and complained of a tightness in my stomach. And while travelling around Europe with Claude, I was frequently more tired than usual. Although I attributed this to our motorcycle journey, now that we were home, I decided to have a complete medical examination.

My doctor, who had been a missionary in China, had examined me externally when I visited her about my stomach. However, she had not wanted to give me an internal examination then because I was "not married." At the time I was very naive about my physiology and accepted her decision.

Since I now was officially married, the doctor did a thorough internal examination. It was a great shock when she discovered a large tumour on my ovaries. When she announced, "You have cancer," it came as a complete and overwhelming shock. I was unable to comprehend the seriousness of ovarian cancer. Claude was devastated, and more loving than ever. I immediately pictured a dreadful death of decay. How could I ever control my fright? I had never felt I needed a God, but now I began to pray silently. Eventually, the doctor's other words sank in, and I began to grasp the meaning of the phrase, "Perhaps it's curable."

The doctor immediately booked me for an operation, which she would perform under the supervision of a specialist. She felt that this surgery would remove all of the cancer cells, but that some further treatment was needed for prevention.

· · ·

After the surgery, I woke up gradually and tried to orient myself to strange surroundings. No one was around. I was lying on a high hospital stretcher bed. My eyes moved to a sign that said "CANCER CLINIC" in bold letters. I couldn't take my eyes off it. My mind said, "You will die of cancer and you're only 32!" I began to feel sorry for myself. Why should this happen to me—just recently married and returned to Vancouver after several years of fascinating work overseas? Our life was just beginning— we wanted kids. Now I had ovarian cancer.

There's something shattering about that word "cancer." Always you expect to hear it connected with someone else—never with yourself. Even when I was told there might be a possibility of malignancy, I refused to consider it. The days passed and gradually a change crept through me. The initial shock was over and instinctively I began to search for a way to go on living. Claude said, "It's a blessing the thing is discovered and treatment has started." I privately consoled myself by saying that at the very worst, I still had several years to live. I resolved to make them the best possible years for both of us. A rush of love swept through me as I appreciated that if this had happened last year, I would have had to face it alone.

With a new understanding and a soul-shaking appreciation, I looked back on my life and realized that it had been good. In the hours that followed, I lay back in bed and remembered the many wonderful experiences and the friendship and love of so many people that had been mine. Eventually I began to appreciate that had this threat not come, I probably would have gone on taking life, health, and love for granted. I slowly realized that this pain might actually result in a wiser outlook and more fulfilling life.

With these thoughts in mind, I began the post-surgical phase of treatment. There was no chemotherapy in those days. Instead, radioactive gold was flown from Chalk River, Ontario, to Vancouver. It was injected through a tube into my uterus. My body was marked like a checkerboard, and a Geiger counter was used to monitor the spread of the gold throughout my abdomen. Later—just to be sure they got all the cancer cells—a cobalt bomb was shoved up my rear end. Six months of compulsive vomiting followed my return home from the hospital. After the violent vomiting had subsided, the doctor said there was no sign of further cancer, but tests would continue for 10 years. And, as if the recovery from cancer treatment wasn't hard enough, losing my ovaries meant the onset of menopause, with the hot flashes, emotional effects and so on.

Through all of it, Claude was more worried than I was. He put up with a lot at that time, all the while providing loving care—and protection from the hospital, which he did not trust. He tried to cross the prohibited radioactive zone to hold me. He complained loudly about hospital errors that had added to my shock. His love supported me over the following weeks while I tried to knit a pair of green socks to leave him as a wifely souvenir. His gift, however, of an Australian budgie that shrieked, "Hello baby, want a kith?" I could have done without.

Claude wasn't the only one who was worried about me. My sister, nurse Betty, moved with her family from Edmonton to Vancouver to be near me. Years later I realized that ovarian cancer is nearly always fatal, and that Betty had moved because she believed I was dying. I realized how very fortunate I was to be alive.

When you are sick, it's interesting how the little pleasures of life become important. I began to enjoy each precious day. Spring grass and flowers leapt at me joyously. Mozart was unbelievably beautiful. Friends were valued in a new way. I recall how eternally grateful I was to my friend, Cleta Herman, who came to the house and washed my hair for me while I lay in bed—one of the things you really appreciate when you are sick.

The shock of learning that I had terminal cancer, the trauma of the operation and treatment, and the weeks of vomiting which followed left me weak and exhausted. On one occasion, when I felt up to it, Claude took me to a party of Neighbourhood House colleagues. I remember getting ready to go, dressing my emaciated body in a black cocktail dress from Red Cross days. Given my physical condition and my sombre attire, I imagine the effect was funereal rather than celebratory, but it was great to be welcomed back.

Claude was a devoted caregiver. But while he worried about me, I was impatient that he wasn't out job-hunting. One day I snapped at him, telling him sharply that he should be out working. He left the house in silence. I later realized how I must have hurt him, and felt very guilty. After a long struggle to find work, Claude bought a small radio shop and started his own business. Soon I would begin to work in community development. I realized that despite our many differences, our love could weather life's problems.

One night Claude picked up one of those half-finished green socks and said, "That's a bloody-looking mess if I ever saw one. Anyway, Luv, I'd rather have you than the socks." Many years later, when I was retiring as a Member of Parliament, I came across the unfinished sock and I remembered this time as a major turning point in my life.

This life-threatening experience changed me profoundly. It resulted in my valuing life as I never had before. My relationship with Claude deepened, and his love and loyalty became more important than his irritating behaviour. My sister Betty and I also became much closer, and I loved her children. She became my supportive friend for the rest of her life.

Recovery, with Substitute Children

As time went on, we moved from survival mode to working for recovery. Claude was busy with his radio repair business, and I had returned as program director at Alexandra Neighbourhood House (called "The Big Pink" by teens because of its paint colour). We both worked long hours.

In 1960, Claude and I bought a two-bedroom bungalow in our

Baby Margaret Learoyd, born in Brockville, Ontario, July 17, 1925.

Mom and Dad, Bill (before he went to war), Margaret (in the difficult teens), Betty (the baby), and Ted (another middle child). Our car horn tooted "Cayuga."

Taking a break with Canadian patients, whom I took shopping for presents before they left Kure, Japan for home.

I served as a Canadian Red Cross worker attached to Commonwealth troops.

Mary, Claire and Jackie camping in the Outback of Australia, heading for Alice Springs, where we ate roasted goanna for breakfast.

Hitchhiking in the Queensland rainy season, where flooded creeks meant we had to push our friends' caravan through the mud.

Margaret and Claude with nephew Billy in Vancouver.

I married Australian
Claude Mitchell in
Vienna in 1957 after
a hectic romance in
three countries.

Refugees outside Brigittaspital Refugee Camp,
where I worked as part of a Canadian Red Cross team.

With Lil Reid
Smith, my long-time
assistant and "boss,"
on the steps of the
constituency office
(at East Hastings and
Penticton Street).

With SPOTA leaders Mary Chan (L) and Bessie Lee.

Bob Mandeville and Jack Allen showing me around Adanac Housing Co-op.

Meeting with an African refugee to help him prepare
for his appeal to remain in Canada.

new neighbourhood, East Vancouver, for $9,000, including appliances. We paid off the mortgage one year later. We raised up the house and completed a family room, bedroom, and bath in the basement. Many friends and family used this suite over the years.

We lived on my salary while Claude reinvested in his Davie Street business, eventually expanding it to include second-hand rental TVs and furniture. His customers continued to include the homeless alcoholics and lonely guys who needed a hangout and used Claude's address. A Russian immigrant named Sergei serviced TVs and provided lots of colour. Claude continued working six days a week and eventually bought several properties, which increased in value over the years. Then he started a motorcycle shop near our home. This gave him a summer business to balance winter TV rentals, and a free motorcycle to ride.

When I was in my late thirties, Claude and I started to talk about the possibility of adopting children. We both loved kids, although our experience with them was quite different. From the time I was a teenaged baby sitter to my time as a group worker, I had always enjoyed working with children, and I related to them easily. In his earlier days in Australia, Claude had built a carousel (merry-go-round) and followed the sun from Sydney to Cairns while entertaining kids. When he first arrived in Vancouver, he had lived with his brother's three preschool kids and usually had redheaded Billy following him when he came to visit me. He teased kids with corny jokes and they obeyed his orders.

Despite our eagerness to expand our family, we realized that until my ten-year probation period passed, my health was still potentially in jeopardy. At one point we considered applying as a couple to run a teen group home, but fortunately my friend at the YWCA was wiser than we were and dissuaded us. I was hurt, but later realized that Claude and I had different approaches to child-rearing. Gradually we found other ways to express our love of children.

Ultimately, Claude and I simply enjoyed the children around us, and didn't spend a lot of time regretting that we had not given birth to them. Claude was like a father to our neighbour Diana Armstrong's kids, Marion, Julie, and David. Diana, a single mother, was Claude's bookkeeper, and over the years he helped her in many ways. He used to take David to motorcycle events and David told his mom that he really liked Claude's coffee (it was laced with scotch). Later on, Claude gave both girls away at their weddings.

Claude also augmented his time with children by joining the Big Brothers Association, and, over the years, was assigned three Little Brothers. The first, Alan, was one of eight siblings living with a single mom on welfare. Alan didn't know who their fathers were. Our little house seemed like a palace to him and he soon brought his younger brother to share the food, proudly telling him how to use a knife and fork.

John, Claude's second charge, was a Little Brother only for a short time. He was bright and responsive, but he was a bed wetter, and his domineering mother made him sleep on a foul mattress to punish him. She resented outsiders, and John and Claude's relationship was short-lived.

Darcy, Claude's third "Little" Brother, was a six-foot-tall teenager. He was likeable, but quite irresponsible. Claude often had to rescue him from scrapes. Finally he got into serious trouble and ended up in Brannan Lake School for Boys on Vancouver Island. We visited him there several times. Darcy was probably too old to change his behaviour, but he remained Claude's friend, dropping in on us periodically over the years.

I developed a close relationship with my sister Betty's kids, often visiting with them on Saturdays when Claude was working. We enjoyed family picnics on our patio, especially when Dad and my stepmother Helen and the Aunts visited, and we held happy winter gatherings in our family room where the kids often put on shows, making good use of the costume box.

Whatever lingering regrets we might have had over not being able to have children of our own slowly faded as Claude and I looked to our future. Change was in the air, and I pondered how I might become part of a movement that would ultimately improve the lives of disadvantaged children and their families.

The Squatters' Shack and the Gulf Islands

One day Claude told me that he had bought me a waterfront cabin. He led me down a mountain and over the railway tracks to a shack built on piles over the high tide mark near Second Narrows (now Ironworkers

Memorial) Bridge. It was one of the squatter's shacks on the south side that were due to be torn down when jurisdictional ownership was decided.

We caught crabs and cooked them on the deck and enjoyed our neighbours, interesting characters living on pensions with no amenities like running water. Although Harry Rankin was their lawyer, eventually they, and we, were forced out, and the community was burned to the ground. On the day that my sister Betty and I and her family decided to take a cruise up Burrard Inlet, her daughter Jane, who was six and had loved the shack, saw the fire on shore and realized that the shack was gone. She was broken-hearted. . . .

On impulse, one weekend we decided to explore Salt Spring Island, one of the beautiful Gulf Islands. Claude headed for Welbury Point as if he knew it. He left me in the car (in his usual Aussie chauvinistic style) and went inside the house. After some time he came out with another man who I could tell was likely an Aussie because he was also wearing shorts, a Hawaiian shirt, and was in bare feet. It was Walter Mailey, who came from Claude's home town, and whose children had ridden on Claude's merry-go-round in Australia. His wife, Shirley, was a Salt Spring Islander. She and I became close friends, defending ourselves from the two macho Aussies. They had two young sons whom we loved.

The Maileys invited us to camp at the campground they owned, and then found us cabin space and eventually a trailer. Betty's kids loved to come to Welbury. We all enjoyed Saturday clambakes and island life. Eventually we bought a lot nearby and moved our trailer onto it. We also had a geodesic dome, which Betty and her husband Jack had built. Many friends and family visited, using the dome until, after much use, it finally disintegrated.

All things are bound to change in time, but I was really very sad when Shirley was diagnosed with cancer and died a year later. Then her oldest son, Norman, was killed in a car accident. Walter lost heart in the business, drank excessively, and left much of the work to his younger son, Bruce. When Walter ultimately returned to Australia and then remarried, I adopted Bruce as my godson.

I loved the ferry trip through the Gulf Islands—the arbutus trees, shell beaches, eagles and blue herons, and occasional whales and dolphins. This love affair with island life continued when, in the '80s, Claude decided to buy a property with a house on Mayne Island. He was not feeling well and needed a more comfortable place. Although I didn't realize it at the time, we would subsequently learn that he was experiencing the first signs of colon cancer. He later told me he wanted me to be closer so I could visit with Betty, who by then lived on Saturna, the southernmost of the Gulf Islands.

Family Visitors and Marital Stress

Over the years Claude visited Australia frequently to see his mother. I went with him twice and she came several times to visit us. She was a great character who dressed flamboyantly and talked continuously. We laughed a lot, and she taught me things, like watching for BCBs ("Bloody Copper Bastards") when we were out driving. On one visit she came with her boyfriend, Billy, on a champagne flight. Carrying two fur coats, she fell backwards down the airport escalator. She immediately called for airport security and had them push her in a wheelchair to complain to the top authorities. "Mom" and Billy loved the pubs and hated the isolation on Salt Spring.

We had other visitors too. My two "maiden aunts"—Aunt Hilda and Aunt Alma—often came west to visit us, bringing love and laughter. After his stroke, Dad came with his new wife, Helen, who had been our English teacher, and he enjoyed his four Speers grandchildren. Betty went home to nurse him before he died while I babysat her kids. (Two years later I invited Helen on a trip to the UK, a tour of Scandinavia, and to a conference in Helsinki. It was a new and exciting experience for her.) Another regular visitor was Dr. Joan Waterfall, who had lived with us for a year when I was ill and her son Malcolm was a baby. (Claude was Malcolm's godfather.) We visited Joan after she returned to England, and she liked to visit BC.

Looking back, I realize that Claude's and my relationship was definitely not conventional, and I am sure many people wondered about us. Sometimes, so did I. I often resented Claude's macho Australian attitudes that were only partly a pose. I often felt tension building inside me when he refused to compromise. Gradually I learned to fight back (which was excellent preparation for life in politics).

As time went on, it bothered me that Claude and I rarely saw my old friends. I especially missed Cleta Herman and Joyce Fitzpatrick, who had trained with me in Toronto. At the same time, Claude made many new friends who became "his" friends more than "our" friends. I continued to get together with friends from work and community, and often went to Salt Spring Island with friends or family when Claude was working. And so we compromised over the years.

However, I found Claude's domineering attitudes very difficult at times. One example was his insistence that I should do the dishes immediately after dinner, when I was tired and wanted to visit with friends. (He often did the dishes himself, but never when we had visitors—that would have ruined his macho image.) One day I went with him to a warehouse and saw a dishwashing machine. I decided to buy it, and paid the salesman. When Claude discovered my "insubordination," he insisted that my cheque be returned. I was furious, and continued to argue about this unfairness. I soon figured out that what he really didn't like about my buying the machine was that it wasn't his idea.

Another source of occasional acrimony was the car. When I was working at the Family Services agency in Vancouver, I worked at one side of the Burrard Street Bridge, and Claude's business was on the other. We had only one car between us, and we were supposed to be taking turns with it. One snowy, cold day I left to meet Claude at the store. I had to walk across the bridge in a blizzard. When I arrived at his store I was really angry, and in front of his mates who worked there said, "I don't see why I can't have the bloody car once in a while." There was a long silence. Finally I heard this voice from the back of the shop, which said, "You *had* the car." (I had forgotten!) He was very good at using those long silences to get his point across.

Another of our continuing disagreements was over my desire to move to a new house that would be near the water in Vancouver East. We looked at a few homes we could afford, but always Claude refused to move, resisting anything that he considered "middle class." Although I sometimes became very frustrated by Claude's domination, and on one occasion seriously considered separating, I realized that I, too, was very strong-minded. However, I was usually the one to back down or to compromise. At the same time, I appreciated Claude's loyalty and love.

He was always there when I needed him, and he helped many people.

Claude especially loved meeting new people, and usually regaled them with stories of our romance and marriage in Vienna. And when we visited old friends like the Maileys on Salt Spring Island, we had a lot of laughs. He was proud of my work in the community, and urged me to enter politics in 1977. He continued to be my staunch supporter for the rest of his life.

The People's Republic of China

In 1973 I was honoured to be included in the first Canadian women's group to visit the People's Republic of China. I was particularly interested in learning more about the Chinese Revolution and the "New China." I became engrossed in and very moved by this intense experience, which has stayed with me ever since.

My friend Jackie Van Campen (nee Robitaille), who had been with me on my trip to the Outback of Australia, joined me on this trip to China. Our group included women journalists, community activists, university professors, and assorted feminists. We were all guests of the Chinese government, which provided us with two wonderful tour leaders. In preparation for the trip I had read Chairman Mao's Little Red Book, the morality of which reminded me of the Sunday School classes of my childhood.

Our trip took place during a very historic time—China was in the midst of the Cultural Revolution. Although we were protected from any violence, which certainly was occurring, we realized that we were going to selected demonstration sites and that the Revolutionary Committee leaders who hosted us in each community were committed Maoists with a propaganda-based agenda. However, that said, we saw many positive developments.

After a few days in Canton, we travelled north from the rice fields and water buffalo of the sub-tropical south, through industrial Wuhan with its famous Yangtse Bridge built by "the People," and detoured briefly to visit the Norman Bethune Peace Hospital in Shijiazhuang. Finally we reached the cold, grey, sandy area of northern China to see life on a rural commune.

Revolutionary leaders stressed self-reliance, a healthy lifestyle, and adherence to Marxist principles. Revolutionary Committee leaders hosted us in each community, describing horrors of olden times and post-revolution achievements of the present regime. I was particularly interested in Chinese medicine. Acupuncture, which Canadian doctors rejected, was used for many purposes in China, including surgery and even in the treatment of mental illness, such as schizophrenia.

Extended families lived in crowded conditions, sharing cooking facilities. Community day care and canteens were available for working mothers, and grandparents helped in the community. The communist government established economic goals, set low national wage levels, and rationed basic food. I was amazed that a nation of more than 750 million people appeared so healthy. There were few cars at that time and even a bicycle was too expensive for most families. People were disciplined by their peers, and some attended "wrong thinking" sessions to reform their minds.

On rural communes, people farmed collectively and developed local industries and services to be self-reliant. In the remote, barren northern regions, survival was difficult. Trees had to be planted in deep holes to protect them from the desert winds. Pigs lived underground!

In Shanghai we visited a day care centre unannounced. The children were seated around tables listening to a story told by one child. The supervisor told us that this child was telling the others that they must "serve the people like Dr. Norman Bethune." Bethune, our Canadian doctor who had accompanied Mao Zedong on the Long March, was almost as famous and beloved it seemed as the Chairman himself.

Our tour leaders arranged for frequent entertainment, including Chinese opera and dance—but only those that were politically approved. We visited the Great Wall, the Ming Tombs, and the Great Hall of the People in Tiananmen Square. The food was marvellous, and we enjoyed the contrast of northern and southern cuisines.

The clapping school children always warmly welcomed their "Canadian aunties." They also sang to us. On one occasion the children asked us to reciprocate by singing a Canadian song for them. There was a long blank silence until in desperation we remembered "Alouette." Teenagers combined farm work with their schoolwork, and when they left school they were sent to a remote area to "serve the people."

Looking back, I realize how naive and protected we were from the violence and deprivation of the Cultural Revolution that was taking place. Intellectuals were being victimized by young members of the Red Guard, and party members controlled most people's lives. I was impressed, however, with some of Mao's teachings. He said, "Men and women hold up half the sky." Unfortunately, this rule did not seem to apply at higher levels of the bureaucracy. With the escalating population threatening China's future, late marriages and small families were encouraged. We were not told of the "one-child family" policy, which, because of its limitations, led to discrimination against girls and led to abortions and deaths of female babies.

. . .

In the communities we visited we were impressed by extensive building of new housing, productive full employment, comprehensive day-care, improving incomes and living standards, and the many self-help community services. The policy of decentralization, self-reliance, and participation of people in their neighbourhood governments was typical. We came back to Canada remembering a nation of happy, alert faces, children bubbling with health, and a feeling that social commitment and involvement were everywhere.

Although I was not converted to Marxism, my belief in a socialism that shared resources fairly, promoted equality, and which encouraged education and healthy living, strengthened after my month in China.

SECTION 2

Community Development

CHAPTER 6

Pioneering Community Development

When it finally sank in that I was indeed going to live, and I was beginning to get my strength back, my thoughts turned to work, and I began to assess my social work career. I had always enjoyed working with people, but I realized much of it involved superficial activities. I now wanted to become more involved in social change. Band-aid solutions were not good enough. I thought about the community development work I had done with refugees in Vienna, and wondered how I could use my experience there to help people in Vancouver.

Politics in Vancouver

While Trudeaumania raged in Ottawa and across the country, provincial politics in BC were also changing. During the '60s, a few Social Credit (Socred) MLAs, like Grace McCarthy, MLA for Vancouver's Little Mountain, were supportive of citizen activities in constituencies as long as they were non-partisan. NDP MLAs like Bob Williams actively supported citizen groups in Vancouver. Another MLA, Norm Levi (who later became NDP Minister of Social Services) led an action movement of progressive workers, The Action Slate, to democratize the boards of social agencies and United Community Services. Unions were forming in the private non-profit sector and the Vancouver Municipal and Regional Employees Union (now the Vancouver Municipal, Education and Community Workers) was becoming more militant.

Then in 1973, after 20 years in power, W.A.C. ("Wacky") Bennett's Socred Party was defeated by the NDP, led by Dave Barrett. Claude took out Canadian citizenship to celebrate, and I became active in the NDP. Our two MLAs from Vancouver East, Bob Williams, Minister of Forestry, and Alex Macdonald, Justice Minister, were powerful Cabinet members.

During the short three years the NDP was in power, much progressive legislation was passed, involving labour, forestry, and agricultural land protection. Major reform of social services by Minister of Social Services Norm Levi resulted in the establishment of the Vancouver Resources Board (VRB).

What happened at that time was that both private and public social service agencies were amalgamated under the VRB to provide a range of services, and workers were decentralized as teams to local communities. I became involved in organizing local Community Resource Boards (CRBs). Later I was hired as a CRB manager.

Vancouver city politics had also changed dramatically during the late '60's when The Electors Action Movement (TEAM) was formed to defeat the right-wing Non Partisan Association (NPA) and bring about progressive changes in city government. TEAM was a coalition of Liberals, some Conservatives, and a few NDP activists, including Mike Harcourt, Darlene Marzari, and myself.

What contributed to these changes in Vancouver was the activism of grassroots organizations such as Vancouver Cool Aid, Inner City Services Project headed by Max Beck (whose colourful bus was used by many groups), the Vancouver Inter Project Tenants Council, the Downtown Eastside Residents Association, and many other neighbourhood organizations. Workers on federal OFY (Opportunities For Youth) grants and volunteers from the Company of Young Canadians (CYC) assisted. Although each group operated independently, they came together to provide mutual support. A city-wide people's movement was emerging.

Tom Campbell, the NPA Mayor of Vancouver (and a developer), hated the hippies and young people who had flocked to Vancouver from across Canada. Kitsilano's Fourth Avenue was the counter-culture hangout of the pot smokers, while Cool Aid and Inner City Projects provided outreach services. Mayor Campbell was furious when community activists, led by Ray Chouinard of Cool Aid, set up an alternative City Council, and we all sat on the City Hall floor to provide people power. (Tom actually wanted to impose the new War Measures Act to rid the downtown of hippies!)

In 1968, TEAM won three seats on City Council. Art Phillips, Walter Hardwick, and Brian Calder had been elected. We were trying to take as many seats as possible away from the NPA, so I ran for Parks Board. Although I was unsuccessful, I enjoyed campaigning. In 1972 Art Phillips became Mayor, and seven TEAM aldermen were elected with him, including Darlene Marzari, who had been a social planner for the City. Under Ray Spaxman, Vancouver's new City Planner, and Maurice Egan, head of the new Social Planning Department, more support was given to citizen involvement in planning.

The most outspoken alderman during the '60s and '70s was Harry Rankin, a feisty East End lawyer who was the sole COPE (Coalition of Progressive Electors) member on Council for many years. By 1980 Harry had been joined by Bruce Yorke, Bruce Erickson, Libby Davies, and Pat Wilson to form a strong, progressive Council. I was especially pleased that Bruce Erickson and Libby were elected because I had worked with them when they were very effective organizers with the Downtown Eastside Residents Association (DERA). It was an exciting time for the Strathcona community in terms of institutional change. I really enjoyed working with people in the community.

However, despite some progressive movement at City Hall, by the '70s it was apparent that TEAM was no longer the "team" we hoped it would be. When the party no longer supported a full Ward System (which would have given more representation to the East Side), I realized TEAM was becoming too conservative, and resigned. Mike Harcourt and Darlene Marzari resigned as TEAM aldermen and ran as independents for City Council. In 1978, they were both elected again, and Mike became Mayor in 1980.

As with other urban action movements across Canada, TEAM disbanded in the early '80s. It was the end of an era. Gordon Campbell, who had worked for Mayor Art Phillips, reactivated the conservative agenda of the NPA, was elected Mayor of Vancouver, then went on to run successfully for provincial leadership of the BC Liberal Party in 1991. Neo-conservatism was spreading, not only in the US, but in Canada too.

During these years of change (in the 1980s), Local Area Planning had been implemented in Vancouver. Ernie Hill, an outstanding planner employed by United Way of Vancouver, introduced this policy in 1965; it divided Vancouver into 22 Local Areas for co-ordination of services and community development. This continued to be used by the city as the basis for City of Vancouver social planning and later by the province for Community Resource Boards. I had pioneered community development in the Area Development Project from 1964 to 1968.

Shared federal and provincial funding under the Canada Assistance Plan (CAP) opened the door to many possibilities, including major social reforms in Vancouver. These reforms helped alleviate poverty and strengthened communities. CAP funding became available for community development workers, and the city's social planners asked the Neighbourhood Services Association to establish a separate Department of Community Development. I became interim director. Having little interest in administration, however, after a short time I returned to grassroots community organizing, which was more satisfying (and more fun).

Changing Direction—Area Development Project

By the mid-'60s I had rejected traditional social work. I was convinced that a new approach was needed to empower citizens and democratize services. I resented social work's problem-focused treatment of people as "clients," diminishing their pride and potential as "citizens." There were too many unco-ordinated specialized agencies, and institutional reform was badly needed.

In the Neighbourhood Houses where I worked, we developed a Joint Family Services Project, a team approach to helping troubled families. I was a case worker for a year or so at Gordon Neighbourhood House and at Family Services agency. This also was too treatment-focused for my taste, although I learned a lot about case work through this project. I didn't know it at the time, but I was ready for a change.

When I had been given leave from Alexandra Neighbourhood House in 1957 to work in a refugee camp in Vienna, my life changed, and so did my approach to social work. This experience in Vienna added to my growing conviction that I wanted to put my social work efforts into community development rather than treatment. The opportunity arose in 1969 to add a new dimension to Vancouver's Area Development Project (ADP), an inter-agency initiative set up by United Community Services (UCS, now United Way of the Lower Mainland) to integrate and decentralize services to troubled families. I was seconded from the Neighbourhood Services Association to work on the ADP.

I proposed selecting the Riley Park Area, which contained Little Mountain Housing Project, as a demonstration neighbourhood for community development. I was hired as the Director of Neighbourhood Services and as the community development worker in the Riley Park Area.

The Red Door—Neighbourhood Services

Riley Park is an old residential neighbourhood adjacent to Queen Elizabeth Park, one of Vancouver's most beautiful tourist attractions. It is also home to the city's first public housing project. It was in this area of Vancouver that I pioneered the use of community development as an effective approach in working with people, to alleviate personal and family problems and to help them achieve their aspirations for a better community. It was here that community development as a social work approach had its Vancouver beginnings.

The Area Development Project was a research project, but it was difficult to define research goals for community development. I was working intuitively and wanted community people to define what they needed. I was given three years to help residents to organize. At one point when I was talking about "community cohesion," the ADP researcher said to me, "Margaret, you can't measure change by a warm feeling in the pit of your stomach." Having a project time-line also created pressures.

Since we had not been asked to intervene, I first had to obtain sanction from the local community. Brock School personnel were very helpful, introducing me to local people. Assisted by a team of social work students, I interviewed key individuals who were active in the community, including tenants and PTA members. People welcomed us, and most felt that children's activities were a priority.

Little Mountain Public Housing in Riley Park was viewed as a kind of ghetto by the larger community, and public housing tenants felt like second-class citizens. I joined in the campaign for a community centre by helping the Riley Park Community Association to organize.

I worked from a tiny storefront, which became known as The Red Door. It became a people place where folks dropped in for coffee, a chat, or to discuss community concerns and plan action. Several social work students helped to lead groups for kids with special needs who were referred from Brock School.

The Red Door became well known locally, and also in the federal Department of Health and Welfare. On one occasion R.A.J. Phillips, the Director of Welfare Grants, came to visit. While I was showing him around our humble office, suddenly the hot water tank burst, and the dignified "RAJ" was put to work holding the leak. Years later I met Mr. Phillips at his home in Ottawa. He looked at me strangely for a moment, then suddenly the light dawned. "You are The Red Door!" he said.

Following the UCS Local Area Planning model, I helped to organize an Area Resources Council of professional workers. (I later concluded this should not be the role of a CD (community development) worker, who should instead work primarily with local residents.)

I started to attend meetings of the Little Mountain Tenants Association (LMTA), which, under the leadership of Sue Trutch and Dorothy Thomas, began to strengthen and develop much-needed programs like a Tot Lot, a study group, and community events. The executive welcomed me and I played a consulting and facilitating role, encouraging public housing tenants to take action on community problems, including developing the kinds of services they wanted in their neighbourhood. I was pleased when the tenants began to confront public housing authorities, sought housing improvements and achieved a greater say in housing policies. They sometimes joined with tenants from other public housing projects to have more impact and gain power.

MOMS—More Opportunities for Mothers

Many of the people I worked with were single mothers who felt trapped on welfare. They lacked education and work experience, were unable to afford daycare (the term has evolved from two words into one), and faced the constant pressures of poverty while trying to raise their kids. We decided to tackle the barriers, starting with daycare. I actively encouraged mothers to organize and provided support and advice. We had fun developing strategies to make social agencies more responsive.

We decided to call a meeting of the heads of welfare, housing, and family agencies. We also included the local Socred MLA (Grace McCarthy) and the NDP MP (Grace MacInnis) as our allies. These guests were seated at the front of the room and asked to listen while one woman after another described her family situation and the barriers that prevented her from getting off welfare. Under the sympathetic eyes of the two women politicians, and confronted by determined "clients," each agency director committed to solving these problems. Afterwards, I helped to mobilize resources. The Lutheran church offered space, and a new childcare centre was initiated with the help of volunteers from the National Council of Jewish Women. City Social Services later broadened coverage to pay for childcare costs.

Institutional change was beginning to happen. The women were proud of their achievements and began to realize they could demand that their rights be respected. A MOMS (More Opportunities for Mothers) group was formed with representation from different housing projects.

Tenant Action and Youth Work

My role now was to encourage tenants and Riley Park residents to work together. It helped that I had a close relationship with the Brock School PTA Chair, who also was active in the Riley Park Community Association. In the fall, a community protest began against the Parks Board decision to cut back on plans for much-needed community meeting rooms in the community centre in favour of an expensive ice rink, which most kids would not be able to afford. Unfortunately, the community lost this battle. Then the LMTA hosted an All Candidates Meeting. Out of this came a commitment from the newly elected MP to work for federal funding for facilities for this public housing community. The tenants were becoming skilled change agents who were enjoying a growing sense of citizen power.

Tenants were concerned about high rents, and I helped a few to organize an open meeting to share concerns. Along with tenants from other projects, they prepared a brief and sent it to the Minister of Housing, to elected representatives, and to government agencies. This brief influenced federal rent revisions and gained tenants considerable prestige. Democracy was beginning to work, and the attitudes of bureaucrats were changing. They were becoming more respectful as tenants gained more power. I was proud of their guts.

This action was also the first step toward the formation of the Vancouver Housing Inter Project Council (VHIPC), which had delegates from all housing projects in the city. This group soon became recognized as the official body for negotiations with the Vancouver Housing Authority and with governments. I worked with this group, along with Nora Curry, who would replace me as community worker when the ADP was phased out. Bill Cross, a Skeena Terrace tenant, became a very active Chair of VHIPC and remained so for many years. Working with the federal government, this organization achieved many changes in public housing policy, including changes in rent structures. VHIPC also held annual tenant conferences for planning and celebrating achievements. As a result of their efforts, public housing management became more accountable to the tenants.

. . .

Many other developments took place in Riley Park during the next two years when Youth Worker Doug Purdy was added, along with a new team of students. Stan McLarty, the Brock School Principal, pointed out the need for a Study Club for under-achieving students. LMTA allowed their meeting room to be used, and individual tutors from UBC helped nine students make amazing progress. The LMTA pressured the Housing Authority to provide space and build a Tot Lot during the summer.

By now our Youth Worker had involved many troubled teens and they organized a very successful Community Carnival, bringing a wide range of groups together. A large program for teens was organized at Tupper High School in the fall. Community police reported much less delinquency. A Riley Park community identity was developing.

Phasing Out ADP

By the fall of 1966, most programs were operating independently and we ADP workers were no longer needed to initiate developments. I was very proud of the activism Riley Park citizens had developed. Reluctantly I began to withdraw. A co-ordinating committee involving different organizations was now considering becoming a Local Area Council. Local people asked that a community worker continue in Riley Park, and eventually UCS hired Nora Curry. On May 1, 1967 a very successful Awards Night was held to recognize Riley Park citizens and to name Brock School Principal Stan McLarty an Honorary Citizen. Two of the tenant leaders went on to become paid community workers in other neighbourhoods, and one was hired by the Housing Authority.

I went back to ADP headquarters to struggle with writing a report called "The Red Door," knowing we had accomplished a lot, but not having objective research to prove it.

I saw community development as a process to help citizens solve problems, involve citizens in local planning, and develop leadership and self-help programs. I believe the community development worker must be committed to citizen goals and citizen rights, operating in consultative roles to develop people, encourage independence, and organize social action to change government policies.

CHAPTER 7

Community Development Expands

The success of the ADP Demonstration Project at Riley Park convinced city planners, UCS, and Neighbourhood Services Association to request Canada Assistance Plan funding for community development in Vancouver. (This was the first time the federal government had made CAP funds directly available to municipalities.)

Neighbourhood Services CD Department

In 1968 I was hired by the Neighbourhood Services Association to set up a Community Development Department. When requested by a local community, this department hired and deployed community workers to neighbourhoods to help local residents organize and develop their communities. We had learned that it was important to have permission from the local community before meddling in their affairs, so a contract with community organizations confirmed that the community development worker would be accountable primarily to the community.

The story of administrative struggles and the developments that occurred in ten communities is documented in the book I wrote in 1975 in collaboration with my colleagues, called *Don't Rest in Peace—Organize!* The following stories tell of the struggles and the fun we had in several Vancouver communities where we pioneered community development. Funding for community development was provided by the City of Vancouver and was cost-shared by the federal government under the

Canada Assistance Plan for five years. Eventually, NSA hired at least ten other community development workers.

After setting up the Community Development Department, I was not interested in the administrative job and continued to enjoy working with community groups. Geoff Cue became the Director of the NSA Community Development Departments and I went back to the grass roots.

Vancouver Opportunities Program

Riding on the success of MOMS, I proposed the development of the Vancouver Opportunities Program (VOP). It became a publicly funded program for social assistance recipients that was managed by women who were themselves on social assistance. Nora Curry and I worked with key tenant activists to develop a proposal to enable mothers on welfare to work and train part-time in schools, libraries, information centres, and self-help programs while receiving an honorarium. Along with tenant leaders, we travelled as a group to Victoria to lobby the Minister, Grace McCarthy, in her purple office. She was very responsive, and afterwards invited the group to lunch in the parliamentary dining room. Impressed by the grandeur, several of our group ordered steaks, and carried home doggy bags for future meals.

As a result of this lobbying, an Opportunities Allowance of $50 monthly was introduced for women on welfare, allowing many women to do volunteer work in their community with transportation and baby-sitting allowances provided. Later the Opportunities Allowance was raised to $100. Effie Keyes was a miracle worker at adapting policies within the Welfare Department. She stretched, extended, and manipulated funds so that allowances could be increased and eligibility extended.

Over a few years, hundreds of women trained, found work, and went off welfare because of the VOP. Community training programs and a Job Development Project were offshoots of the program. Women worked and trained as aides in schools and libraries as well as in health and childcare programs. Many self-help programs were started. New local information centres, tenant and welfare rights offices, two new food co-operatives, and a tenant management experiment in Little Mountain could not have operated without VOP volunteers. This VOP program was expanded later, had its own office, and was run by VOP graduates. I helped a Men's

Group to organize and develop a Community Workshop (only men who were "unemployable" were eligible for the Opportunities Allowance). I continued as a part-time Neighbourhood Services person attached to the VOP. This was required for city funding, but I suspected the VOP leaders resented this requirement and I became less involved.

The Militant Mothers of Raymur

Raymur Housing Project, located in the Downtown East area, is one of the city's oldest and largest public housing projects. It was imposed on the Strathcona community to replace demolished houses as urban renewal took place. It had no amenities and was often referred to as "the snake-pit" by poor people who felt trapped there and longed to escape.

Children who lived at Raymur Housing Project had to walk across busy railway tracks to go to school. About twelve mothers who previously had been strangers formed a strong group, determined to get an overpass over the railway to protect their kids. Mothers lobbied politicians and city officials for an overpass, but with no results. Finally they decided to take direct action.

For a week, twenty mothers camped in their tents on the railway tracks, stopping train traffic to the Port of Vancouver. Activists from across the city swarmed to applaud and support them. Half of the women agreed to go to jail if necessary, while the other half agreed to look after their kids. Along with other activists, I supported them each day, but we did not interfere with their decisions. My little red car carried a wine bottle and food for refreshment.

Carolyn Jerome, the sister of famous runner Harry Jerome, agreed to be on duty when officials came to serve an injunction to make the protestors desist. Each time they arrived, she tore off up the tracks and they were unable to catch her. Eventually the protesting women were taken to court by the powerful Great Northern Railway, which had several lawyers representing them. The Militant Mothers had none, until a sympathetic lawyer volunteered to represent them as a "Friend of the Court." He eventually won on a technicality. There was great rejoicing! The city agreed to build an overpass.

A strong sense of community resulted from this action, and tenants in Raymur organized many more improvements including a food co-op and recreation programs staffed by people in the neighbourhood. They eventually negotiated to take over the Housing Authority offices, and the Ray-Cam Co-operative Community Centre was built. Nora Curry was their community development worker, and Jean Amos was an active president. (Today the centre still provides a place for youth activities.)

The Unemployed Citizens' Welfare Improvement Council

As a Community Worker hired by Neighbourhood Services Association, I supported poor peoples' movements that were forming in BC and across Canada, including the BC Federation of Citizen Groups. This led to a national Poor Peoples' Conference and the formation of the BC Federation of Anti-Poverty Groups.

Members of the Unemployed Citizens Welfare Improvement Council (UCWIC) in Vancouver were advocates for people on welfare and militant anti-poverty protesters. I helped them obtain the use of an office in a Neighbourhood House where their radical actions often challenged authorities. Once I joined them when they had a sleepover in the welfare office to protest social assistance rates. I enjoyed their fighting spirit. They often took on the welfare establishment. When he was suffering from burnout, I invited one of their leaders, Alex Bonde, a Hungarian immigrant, to take a break and stay in our trailer on Salt Spring Island. I was concerned later when I heard that Alex had gone underground, amid rumours that the RCMP were looking for him. I later learned that he had returned to Hungary.

Amid the serious work we were doing, there was also humour. When the Senate Committee on Poverty came to town, I presented a brief. One of the UCWIC members, named Margaret (Ellen) Mitchell (she always called me "the other Margaret Mitchell"), also made a presentation to the committee. Both were reported in the *Vancouver Sun*. While expressing her outrage over the practice of looking for "men under the bed" (which could affect an individual's access to social assistance funds), she declared, "All social workers are sex perverts." The next day I received countless complaints from social work colleagues who had read the "Margaret Mitchell" quote in the paper, and, being unaware of the name confusion, blamed me for the insult. I kidded them, saying that I thought it didn't hurt for social workers to have a sexier image.

"Your Going Away Party Was a Riot"

I was sad when eventually it was time for me to move on from working with poverty groups to work in other East End neighbourhoods. My pals organized a Chinese dinner at Ming's Restaurant as a farewell. As my friends were making speeches, a party of Allstate Insurance representatives took over a mike and drowned us out. Carolyn Jerome, a leader of the Militant Mothers, asked them to turn down their mike. A second and stronger request in more colourful language was also ignored. Finally one of their group came to our table and said, "We know you people are on welfare, so we will pay your bill if you leave." Walter Grey, a proud Cree, rose to his feet, stared him in the eye, and with great dignity said, "You pup!"

That may have been the last bit of dignity displayed. Bedlam broke out when Allstate "heavies" jumped on "Phil," who had just come out of Crease Clinic at Essondale. Tall Emily Houstis from UCWIC raised a chair over her head in attack. Carolyn went in with both fists flying and then complained, "He hit me." When my husband Claude cracked his Australian stock whip (which he'd brought along for entertainment), it was too much for the poor proprietress, who called the police. We managed to escape before they arrived. Afterwards my pals often said, "Your going away party was a riot, Marg."

CHAPTER 8

Local Area Planning

G randview Woodland Area, centred on Commercial Drive, had long been a settlement community for Italian immigrants. Their children attended Britannia High School, along with Chinese students from adjacent Strathcona and Aboriginal students living in native housing. Commercial Drive had many Italian businesses and held a popular Italian carnival each summer. Italian-speaking ethnic organizations were strong, but there was little overall community participation in this rapidly changing neighbourhood.

I was asked to work in this community part-time to encourage citizen participation in planning for a future multi-service Britannia Centre. Dr. Roger Tonkin from UBC was organizing a new multicultural Community Health Clinic, called REACH, and I worked out of a Neighbourhood Information Centre located in one of the storefronts, which REACH had rented. Although a UCS (United Community Services) planner had already brought together professional workers from schools, health and social agencies to form an Area Resources Council, I was concerned that this approach by non-resident professionals would discourage community people from participating.

Concurrently, a very lively group of high-school students, called ATTAC, had formed. These students campaigned rigorously to pass the city's Five Year Plan, which included funding for expanding Britannia. Their teacher, John Minichiello, was a strong advisor, and Joe Ferrera and Enzo Guerriero were student leaders. Many years later Joe taught at Britannia High School; Enzo became Executive Director of Britannia Centre.

I enjoyed the enthusiasm of the ATTAC group and encouraged them to form a citizens' council for Grandview Woodland. They infiltrated the Area Resources Council, recruited local people to run for election, and organized a takeover, converting the council of non-resident professionals into an Area Council of local residents. This group led the early planning process for Britannia Centre, which, in addition to having an elementary school and a high school, would include recreation facilities and many other community services including a library. Ultimately, Michael Clague replaced me as the full-time community development worker in Grandview Woodland, working on extensive planning for the multi-service Britannia Centre, now a model for North America.

Also during this period, the City of Vancouver was considering a proposal for an east-west freeway that would pass through Grandview-Woodland, Strathcona and the Hastings neighbourhoods. Realizing the gravity of the potential impact on densely populated East End neighbourhoods, community workers helped ATTAC, SPOTA (Strathcona Property Owners and Tenants Association), and other citizen groups to organize a mass protest. ATTAC provided a link to Italian and Chinese parents who spoke little English. Together they circulated petitions, dramatized the issues, and organized busloads of delegations to City Hall whenever there was a hearing about the freeway plan. SPOTA brought busloads of Chinese seniors to city hearings.

Despite the determination of city engineers to have a freeway, wide publicity and intensive lobbying persuaded Vancouver City Council to abandon the idea. This victory resulted in growing solidarity between Local Areas and wider involvement of concerned citizens throughout the East End of Vancouver. In future years, whenever the freeway idea resurfaced at City Hall, local citizens and organizations would immediately rise up against it. People power was achieving important results.

Strathcona Defends Itself

The most interesting community that I worked in was Strathcona, one of Vancouver's oldest neighbourhoods. It is the heart of Vancouver's

Chinese community, adjacent to the Chinatown business district. Other immigrants had moved through Strathcona, leaving behind a scattering of Ukrainian, Russian and Italian families and their cultural centres. In the '60s, urban renewal had destroyed many original family homes and replaced them with two large public housing projects—Raymur on the east side and McLean Park on the west. Their new tenant neighbours had very different values and lifestyles from those of the traditional Chinese families.

By 1969 the remaining homeowners were determined to save their homes from the wrecking ball. Many did not speak English and they were not accustomed to demanding their rights. Darlene Marzari, a perceptive social planner, asked NSA if I could help citizens in Strathcona to organize. I agreed on condition we get a Cantonese-speaking community worker to partner with me.

Darlene introduced me to the Chan family, who were respected leaders in the community. Mr. Chan spoke English and had been a teacher in China. He agreed that people should do something to save their homes. We planned a community meeting, which was held at the Boys' Club. Mrs. Chan spoke little English, but she was a dynamo when it came to activating her neighbours. She recruited so many people that the meeting overflowed the hall. The Boys' Club director acted as interpreter. People spoke with great feeling, and it was agreed that an organization should be formed to fight urban renewal and save their homes. Mr. Chan consented to act as chairman, and both English-speaking and Cantonese-speaking officers were elected. Strathcona Property Owners and Tenants Association (SPOTA), which was to change Canada's housing policy, was born at this meeting.

After the meeting, Darlene Marzari introduced me to Bessie Lee, the mother of eight who became a very effective facilitator and bilingual leader. She also became a life-long friend. Tom Mesic was English chairman, and later Harry Con, who was bilingual (and an active federal Liberal), also became very involved. Block captains were named to keep their neighbours informed and bring them out to meetings, which were always held in both Chinese and English. I assisted in many practical ways. Food was always a tool for livening up SPOTA meetings. I admired the SPOTA strategy of inviting bureaucrats and politicians to Chinese dinners, plying them with scotch, and then charming them into co-operating with SPOTA's requests.

Darlene Marzari, along with Shirley Chan, an SFU student, recruited resource people to assist SPOTA, including Mike Harcourt, a community lawyer. When federal Housing Minister Paul Hellyer came to town, they worked hard to convince his assistants of the need for change. SPOTA prepared a very strong brief and Shirley presented it at the Hellyer Hearing on Housing, claiming that urban renewal was destroying homes and would cause cultural genocide in Strathcona. The Minister was convinced. A new National Housing Act was introduced that would help older communities across the country to rehabilitate homes, not raze them. Strathcona was chosen as a pilot project and the City of Vancouver bureaucrats were told they must plan with citizens.

I gradually withdrew from the work in Strathcona since Cantonese-speaking Jonathon Lau, a social worker who had come from Hong Kong, was now available to help SPOTA develop. He lived in McLean Park and involved many seniors. When federal funds became available for the Strathcona Rehabilitation Project, Jonathon was a key link between the community and Vancouver city planners. Nora Curry also worked for several years with SPOTA to develop housing and a new co-operative. Joe Wai, a community-oriented architect, involved SPOTA members in planning innovative housing that was in keeping with the older neighbourhood and at a density that kept costs affordable.

In addition to rehabilitating older homes, SPOTA introduced many innovations as part of the rehab program, including a community school, a linear park, infill housing (in between existing older homes), and both co-op and strata title units. Bessie Lee encouraged people to work with the wider community. SPOTA was a leader in insisting to City Council that a freeway through their community was simply unacceptable. They joined other communities in the protest at City Hall. When they learned later that city planners were designing a north-south freeway to cut through Strathcona, they immediately protested to City Council and stopped it. As a result, Vancouver is—fortunately—one of the few large cities that has not been completely chopped up by freeways.

I learned much from this experience in Strathcona. I developed an understanding of the history and culture of Chinatown, especially its multicultural aspects, and learned to organize in both languages. I also made many friends. I was honoured to be considered a "Friend of SPOTA" and was always invited to its events.

Hastings Sunrise—Adanac Co-op

Claude and I lived in the Hastings area near Boundary Road, which separates Vancouver and Burnaby. This working-class community is chopped into islands by major traffic arteries. Thunderbird neighbourhood to the south was dominated by the large Skeena Terrace public housing project. Adanac neighbourhood, where we lived, was formerly a mushroom farm and still had undeveloped city lands. The area to the north was dominated by Hastings Street (which was very busy), the Pacific National Exhibition (PNE), and the Port of Vancouver. I became involved in many local activities as a resident and later as a Community Development worker, since there were often conflicts between citizen organizations, and between citizens and city officials.

I enjoyed my Adanac neighbourhood. My neighbours, Buster Foster and Peggy Distefano, and I kept watch over the neighbourhood and often confronted the city. Peggy was an assertive blonde from Liverpool who loved a good fight. Buster, a tough labour man with a soft heart, had worked in the North and then in Vancouver as a machinist. He now fought for seniors. One time he talked Peggy and me into demonstrating outside the Canadian Labour Council Convention for pension reforms.

Our first battle was to support mothers whose kids had to cross Highway 1 to get to school. I encouraged them to form a cordon of people across the freeway, and we stopped suburban traffic from going into the city at rush hour. Supported by our MLA, Bob Williams, we won an overpass.

Peggy led our forays to City Hall, cajoling and seducing city officials in her loud Liverpool accent. She complained to the city about garbage and rats on vacant lands, and the delays in building a strip park, which was promised to separate us from industrial development. She especially loved to challenge the new head city planner, Ray Spaxman, who was also from Liverpool, calling him "Love" in front of his colleagues. We usually got our way because they wanted to get rid of us.

In 1969 we joined with people from other Hastings organizations to protest industrial encroachment into vacant Adanac lands. We launched mass meetings, sent petitions to City Hall, overruled city planners, and won approval from City Council to develop Adanac as a residential community. City planners were instructed to plan with citizens for new housing and amenities. Gradually city engineers and planners realized that they could no longer arbitrarily impose roadways and new developments without the approval of residents.

For their part, citizens began to realize that there was power in having a strong united community voice. Despite political rivalries, the Hastings Sunrise Action Council (HSAC), chaired by Jim Cork, was endorsed as a planning and co-ordinating body with delegates from about fifteen organizations. In 1971 we began an official planning process for the Adanac area. The city lands in the north were designated for co-op housing and the south sector (where we lived) for new infill housing.

After a year we were able to get a grant from CMHC to hire a community architect and planner from Urban Design. In 1972 I began working in Adanac as a Community Development worker. At first this caused some confusion, since previously I had been a volunteer citizen. In addition to handling the necessary administrative tasks, I worked at broadening participation in the Council and helped the Adanac Co-op to organize. More local groups got involved as we supported their issues. We successfully opposed the freeway extension, worked with the Parks Board for improvements to Rupert Park, and supported the protests of Hastings Townsite residents against a hotel development and PNE parking problems.

It was difficult to involve my neighbours in complex planning since many spoke little English (we counted seventeen nationalities on our two streets), were elderly, or worked shifts. Survival was more important to people than future planning. Urban Design set up a planning workshop in my garage, and later we had a trailer on a city lot that served as an information centre and a place to meet. Peggy went door-to-door, inviting people to meetings. When the plans were drafted with some denser housing to make it affordable, people began to get interested. Old-timers wanted family housing only, on 33-foot lots—no seniors' housing or townhouses. At last people came out to meetings and a compromise was reached.

City planners obviously had a different agenda for this area and they resisted citizen planning. At one time they withdrew altogether, and Jim Cork led a delegation to City Council in protest. To resolve this impasse, the city appointed Alderman Mike Harcourt as council's official liaison between the community and the planners to help reduce conflicts and to help them reach a consensus. A compromise was finally reached for the Adanac neighbourhood, but it was several years before infill housing was built.

Led by longshoreman Jack Allen, the Adanac Housing Co-op grew from a fledgling committee to a large organization, and negotiations began with governments. I attended meetings and helped with many of their problems and arrangements. The co-op hired creative architects and developed policies to include low-income tenants. The city agreed to sell Adanac land to the province, which then leased it to the co-op. One hundred and sixty units of affordable housing were built, and a lively new community grew. Later a community hall was added. Lou and Jack Allen were strong leaders over many years. I enjoyed walking through the Co-op to my home and attended many co-op events.

Skeena Terrace Housing Project in the northeast part of Vancouver also needed community development help. Over the years, Skeena had several CD workers, including Marjorie Martin and "Muggs" Sigurgeirson, who later gave outstanding leadership at Carnegie Centre downtown. I often was involved at Skeena. Tenants started Frog Hollow Information Centre and a local newspaper, which eventually moved from Thunderbird neighbourhood to a storefront off First Avenue. We worked from there to hold meetings in all school neighbourhoods to promote a Community Resource Board for the Hastings community. Unfortunately there was a low turnout for CRB elections since no follow-up was done after I moved to work in Strathcona.

Downtown Eastside Residents Association

While I was working as an organizer in Vancouver East neighbourhoods, Bruce Erickson and his partner, Libby Davies, were very active in the Downtown Eastside. Along with Jean Swanson, who became an anti-poverty activist, they helped to organize the Downtown Eastside Residents Association (DERA), involving hundreds of poor people who lived in rooming houses, old hotels, or on the streets. Anna Wong worked with a large group of Chinese seniors who joined protests to City Hall. Libby persuaded City Council to renovate the old Carnegie Library building, and Carnegie Centre, the best-used facility in town, was born. It continues to be a home for many homeless people and others, who drop in each day.

DERA became politically active at every election and was a strong supporter for the left-wing COPE party. This infuriated most of the NPA city councillors. (Later both Bruce and Libby became city councillors, along with Harry Rankin and Bruce Yorke.) Bruce and Libby received a salary through the NSA Community Development Unit, but worked independently. I often joined in the protests downtown and admired the militancy of DERA workers.

Although people in the Downtown Eastside were 100-percent poor and had a high incidence of addiction and involvement in prostitution, they also had a strong sense of community, thanks largely to the efforts of DERA. I resented the stereotyping of downtown residents by the media, which described Vancouver's Downtown Eastside as the worst neighbourhood in Canada.

CHAPTER 9

The Demise of Community Development

After five years of productive community development activity in over ten neighbourhoods, Vancouver City Social Planning stopped funding for all CD workers except for DERA's Bruce Erickson and Nora Curry, who continued working with the Vancouver and District Public Housing Council.

Funding Stops but Organizations Continue

Most citizen organizations were established now and could carry on without outside help. Citizens had developed organizing skills and social-action strategies. They knew how to deal with bureaucracies and demand their rights. Tenants in public housing had a strong city-wide organization that had helped to change many housing policies. The Vancouver Opportunities Program was well established, and hundreds of graduates had trained and found work. Development of Britannia would continue with Michael Clague as Executive Director. Experienced SPOTA members along with Jonathon Lau and Nora Curry would continue to plan innovative housing and monitor the Strathcona Rehabilitation Program, which was well underway. Adanac Co-op was built.

Writing the CD Story: *Don't Rest in Peace—Organize!*

I was hired to write our community development story, *Don't Rest in Peace—Organize!* Colleagues contributed. I also organized a National

Community Development Workshop sponsored by the Canadian Association of Neighbourhood Services. We held workshops in four Canadian cities, bringing together a variety of community workers. The finale was a major workshop held at Montebello in Quebec. My reports documented this two-year project.

Ultimately, I felt my goal of empowering citizens and democratizing services had been achieved, and many wonderful people had been involved. It was truly a rewarding life experience.

Vancouver Resources Board

In 1973, the NDP provincial government undertook major institutional reform of social services. They integrated social agencies under the Vancouver Resources Board and decentralized services under elected Community Resource Boards. I was asked to organize Community Resource Boards in two East End communities, Strathcona and Hastings Sunrise.

In Strathcona, after an amazing bilingual election with the highest turnout of voters in the city, the new Strathcona Resources Board was elected. They hired me as their local CRB Manager of Social Services.

In addition to working with the Community Board and funding community projects, I was an administrator of welfare services for Strathcona. While I enjoyed community contacts, my heart was not in administration. One "welfare cheque day," Patsy George, a co-ordinator, came to look for me. She eventually found me circulating a petition among clients advocating higher welfare rates—perhaps an attempt to relieve my guilt over being a welfare bureaucrat.

When the new Social Credit government was elected in 1975 it was determined to wipe out most of the progressive changes that had been made under the NDP, including community development programs and the Vancouver Resources Board. I was assigned responsibilities for three Local Areas: Strathcona, Grandview, and Hastings. Eventually I was terminated, along with several other known NDP supporters. We hired a lawyer and negotiated a six-month severance pay settlement. The time had come to go into politics.

An Evaluation of Community Development

In a 2004 article entitled, "Margaret Mitchell and the Introduction of Community Development in BC," Roopchand Seebaran, who taught at UBC School of Social Work, wrote:

> *I believe that Margaret Mitchell was moved by both her personal and professional experiences to change the way in which social work was being practised in Vancouver by many of her colleagues. Her experience with ordinary citizens whom she served in various professional roles, and her solidarity with them in confronting struggles they faced, had a profound impact on her.*

He was right.

At the time, conditions in Vancouver were ripe for a shift to community development. People were increasingly optimistic that social change was possible. Those who had previously been left out of community decision-making processes became active and vocal. The extreme conservatism of both the provincial and municipal governments of the day contrasted sharply with the approach of the federal government, which encouraged community involvement through the Canada Assistance Plan, the Company of Young Canadians, and Opportunities for Youth. These factors, along with the rise of a counter-culture which included anti-poverty movements, mobilized people of all ages to take action, achieve results, and become advocates for social change.

My own shift to a community development approach to social work had much to do with how I viewed social services and social workers. I hated the patronizing term "clients" and usually referred to people as "citizens." I advocated for a major overhaul of the social service delivery system to make agencies less self-serving and more supportive of the poor people they were set up to help. And I promoted self-help and self-development opportunities for poor people so that they might take greater control of their own lives. I enjoyed working in local neighbourhoods, helping people to organize, and I am told that my sense of humour and love of fun were contagious.

The following excerpts taken from a presentation I made to the Canadian Conference on Social Welfare in 1970 sum up my approach and my criticisms.

For too long the highest proportion of social service dollars has gone to expensive treatment services and institutional care. We have very little evidence of success, unless it is the fact that we provide employment for a large number of agency executives, unit directors, supervisors, clerical personnel, and maintenance people. And then we must add co-ordinators and use more professional time for co-ordinating meetings, inter-agency case conferences, and records, reports, and referrals between agencies. Is it any wonder little time is left for direct work with people?

Poor people need money rather than services. They want hope for the future and opportunities to do their own thing in their own way. Few want 'rehabilitation' or counselling. At best, social services are necessary amenities that should help provide creative opportunities and resources for self-help and community development. Reorganization and innovative approaches are needed at central as well as at local levels. Many of the old methods and highly specialized techniques simply don't work. Freud was a Victorian and so are we if we see ourselves as analysts rather than activators. Everyone pays lip service and supports the new if they can keep the old ways, too, and get more funds while still holding on to agency identity and established jobs.

If as social workers and board members we honestly think that improvements are needed, shouldn't we become change agents within our own agencies and in our own communities? Instead of fearing activists, people movements, and politics, let's show people that we really care enough to join them in the struggle, even if it means a risk to our own job.

A number of positive changes can be attributed to the shift to a community-based approach to service delivery, and to the efforts of local citizens and community development workers. Citizens were now actively participating in the affairs of their community, and citizen advocacy and social action brought about change. They identified needs, got involved in local planning and program development, and became leaders. Many of the groups, such as area councils, housing co-ops, and anti-poverty groups, got their start then (in the 1960s and early 1970s) and still exist today in one form or another. Some who had never voted in elections became politically involved as a result of their participation in community issues. And people began to make the connection between politics and the conditions in their communities. As a result, citizens made demands and politicians began to pay much more attention to East Side issues.

For their part, social service agencies and organizations became more willing to participate with citizens in joint planning and development activities, modified policies and procedures to facilitate that process, and made their workers more accountable to community members. Generally, social work practitioners in all areas of service began to see the importance of community involvement. Ordinary citizens now had a role in allocating funds for non-statutory community programs. And the ghetto image of public housing projects disappeared as tenants joined with the broader community to improve their neighbourhoods.

Community development workers and citizens involved in community development actions learned a great deal through the process. They learned to listen and to wait for citizens to offer ideas, encouraging and supporting them in their efforts to achieve their objectives; to believe that citizens have the capacity to create solutions which would emerge as people worked together; to develop a strong grassroots organization that is accountable to the larger community; to avoid community dependence on government resources, which can easily be withdrawn; and to use community events, including celebrations, social gatherings, and tangible accomplishments to maintain interest. They also learned the value of using humour and having fun in the process, and when to take a break from the action and get re-energized.

Roop Seebaran wrote:

> So who is this person that so many ordinary citizens, human service professionals and various community leaders admire and hold in such high esteem? Margaret is viewed by many of her colleagues as the person who introduced community development as an effective approach to social work practice during the 1960s in Vancouver. As

a result of her work, citizens developed their own action groups to challenge the existing social service systems and the political structures: to fight for their rights in terms of needed services and resources; to tackle the problems facing their children and families; and to organize community action to address local issues, including the protection of their neighbourhoods.

Citizens who became involved in the various social and political actions during this time were able to achieve substantial change in several areas regarding their personal lives and the development of their community. These included establishing citizen area councils that were formally recognized by public planners, the forming of self-help and support groups for mothers, developing programs and activities for children and youth, causing a pedestrian walkway to be built across a set of railway tracks for safety reasons, and changing federal housing policy from one of urban renewal to urban redevelopment and rehabilitation. Moreover, the persistence and activism of citizens caused human service agencies to become more responsive to the needs of the people and the issues in local neighbourhoods.

It is true that Margaret introduced community development in Vancouver at a time when the approach was already being used with very favourable results in agricultural societies overseas. She was also influenced by contemporary social movements, both in the US and within Canada, such as the counter-culture movements, welfare rights, civil rights, anti-poverty campaigns, and the Alinsky model of social action. But, more than any of these, it is clear that Margaret's personal principles, her passion for social justice, and her belief in the worth, dignity, and capacity of people were the driving forces of her practice.

Thus, she worked on issues that directly affected local people, issues related to poverty, respect, welfare of children, health, education, and recreational activities. She was not afraid of the potential negative consequences to her career as a result of her social action role and her solidarity with citizens. When needed, she did not retreat from challenging systems and institutions which employed her, or that were part of the power structure in the community. She advocated for more responsive social service agencies and for institutional reform of these systems. She embodied the values of the social work profession in carrying out her practice by always being accountable to the community in which she worked.

Reflections on Community Development

Looking back, I realize that we accomplished a great deal in the '70s, helping citizens to organize and develop their communities. Personally I developed in many ways. I became more radical, became a more outspoken advocate, and learned a great deal about the impacts of politics, politicians, and bureaucrats on communities. Along with citizen activists, I enjoyed "shit disturbing" and challenging the powers that controlled people's lives.

When I look back, it is the neighbourhood people whom I remember most—the people who first became active to protest and then to collectively solve problems and make major changes in their communities. Their courage and growth as activists continue to amaze me.

I also maintained a fond bond with other community development workers who were my colleagues. One of them, Nora Curry, became my lifelong friend. We often joked about our contrasting community development roles, which reflected our different personalities. I was usually the more aggressive organizer to enter a community, stimulating and encouraging people to be active, and confronting established power structures. When groups became established, I moved on to new assignments.

Nora was a gentler, quieter person with a will of iron, who was very sensitive and patient. She believed in a non-directional approach encouraged people to develop at their own pace. She was especially skilled at working with public housing tenants in the Vancouver Housing Inter Project Council, who ultimately became housing experts. She was a trainer who helped people to grow.

Nora raised six children during those years, and she worked long hours at low pay. She quietly contributed to innovative planning in Vancouver, such as the plans for a mixed community in False Creek South. Cathy Goldney, a CYC volunteer, worked closely with Nora on many projects.

By 1970, I had rejected the middle-class conformity and many of the conventions that I had been raised in and that were common in the social work profession. Claude's working-class values, his identity with poor people, and his no-nonsense confrontational approach to life had changed me. My world travels had broadened my view of society. Surviving cancer had changed the focus of my life.

As we fought community battles, I became much more politically aware and angry at the injustices so many people suffered. I enjoyed political action and learned new strategies for social change. Eventually this led to my personal interest in running as an NDP candidate in Vancouver East. I was ready for a new chapter.

Politics

CHAPTER 10

Learning the Ropes

I am often asked why I became a politician, and I have no ready answer. Unlike many male colleagues, for me, going into politics was not a long-time ambition or an ego trip. I was not seeking power or publicity, although, as I began to emerge from my shyness, I enjoyed being in the public eye. I knew, as a politician, that I had to sell myself and my beliefs.

Perhaps my political career started in childhood when Dad implanted a sense of egalitarianism and community service in me. Small-town life in Cayuga and experience in groups made me an extrovert (albeit a shy one) who enjoyed people and who often helped in leadership roles. At the University of Toronto School of Social Work, I began to see the value of political action and the need for social change, and I was influenced by progressive professors and radical students. Despite living in conservative Ontario, I was becoming a socialist, although as yet, I had no connection with a political party.

These "radical" tendencies remained dormant until I began to travel in 1953. In Korea I realized the immorality of war and the need to work for peace. In the South Pacific I was intrigued with cultural diversity, and abhorred the racist policies of colonial governments. When I met Claude, he challenged my polite middle-class attitudes and he encouraged me to speak out more directly and with feeling. He also taught me how to fight, to stand up for what I wanted.

I began to identify with working-class people in Vancouver East and supported union activities by visiting local union offices and attending demonstrations to promote jobs. Community development made me much more aware of government policies that were affecting people's lives and the need for anti-poverty programs, social housing, and action to counteract discrimination. I enjoyed political action.

When I was asked to run in Vancouver East, the time was right for me and for the party. I had a supportive husband and no children. Politics became my full-time job, and I was tutored by many experienced New Democrats. I enjoyed the excitement of politics and the challenge of being a woman candidate. I met many interesting people and worked very hard. By 1979, I was addicted.

Becoming a Candidate

The federal riding of Vancouver East stretches from Cambie Street east to Boundary Road, and from the harbour waterfront south to Sixteenth Avenue, including the local areas of Hastings Sunrise, Grandview Woodland, Strathcona, parts of the Downtown Eastside, and parts of Mount Pleasant. All of these areas had a long and active labour tradition, where people took pride in being working class. Although there was also a high incidence of unemployment and poverty in these neighbourhoods, they were strong communities with many active citizen organizations. Most union offices were located in Vancouver East, where many of the members lived and worked.

I loved the changing ethnic mix, which now included Chinese Canadians in Strathcona, Italians and Portuguese in Grandview, and increasing numbers of recent immigrants from China, Vietnam, Korea, and Latin America. Earlier European immigrants and Japanese Canadians had moved away from the area, but still had cultural and historical roots in Vancouver East.

The East End had a proud socialist tradition, and in the past had provided outstanding leadership, both in the BC Legislature and in Ottawa. In 1953 Harold Winch (an electrician by trade) was elected to the House of Commons as MP for Vancouver East and continued in that role for many years, after having long been leader of the provincial CCF. When Harold Winch resigned, he was replaced by labour leader

Paddy Neale, who was defeated by Liberal Art Lee in the 1970s. Angus MacInnis represented the adjacent federal riding of Vancouver-Kingsway and was succeeded by his widow, Grace MacInnis, who was the only female MP in Ottawa at the time and a woman greatly admired.

Bob Williams was a very strong MLA for Vancouver East and right-hand man to Dave Barrett when he became the NDP Premier in 1972. Bob was proud to be from Vancouver East and worked hard for constituents. He was my main advisor when I decided to run for nomination in 1979. He had a strong following of young New Democrats. When they needed someone to "tell me off," Bob was the guy. Although he was intimidating, I usually managed to stand up to him and this helped prepare me to stand up to others. I appreciated his support, and he and Claude were good friends.

By the early 1970s the politics were getting more interesting. The New Democratic Party was making a breakthrough in British Columbia after many years of Social Credit domination. Though I had joined a civic group called TEAM earlier, I soon realized the NDP was where I belonged. I became a member in 1972 when Dave Barrett's government was elected in Victoria.

With Dave Barrett now the Premier and Vancouver East MLAs Bob Williams and Alex Macdonald occupying senior provincial Cabinet positions, these were exciting times. Federally, we had lost the Vancouver East riding to Liberal Art Lee in the Trudeau sweep. Now our troops were very keen to regain this seat that had always been CCF-NDP.

My community work had made me much more aware of the need for government action to create jobs and help low-income people. Prime Minister Trudeau scorned western Canadians and seemed not to know or care about the struggles many families were enduring. I became more openly critical and political in my views. I had gained skills and confidence and was a strong supporter of NDP policies.

I was becoming more and more interested and active in politics, but I was startled nonetheless when one day, out of the blue, Stu Headley, an NDP activist on the Vancouver East Federal Council, asked me to run for the federal nomination. I had never considered politics as a career, and was very ambivalent about the proposal. However, I met with a few of the key players from Vancouver East Provincial NDP Council. They wanted an early start to defeat Art Lee, and thought my community work, especially in the Chinese community, had made me well known and respected, and that I would make a good prospective candidate.

As I considered running, I became more intrigued. Claude was very enthusiastic and thought I would be a great MP, but I wasn't so sure. I didn't think I had the necessary skills and background, but Claude was very keen for me to run. (I learned only recently that he was the one who had first promoted the notion.) I pondered the idea. My community work was ending and I needed new challenges, but could I actually do it?

I knew it would be especially challenging because I would be running in Vancouver East, which had large Italian and Chinese populations, and it wasn't common in either of those societies for women to assume political leadership. And of course even within our own party, there were those who had their own reservations.

I had good support on the Vancouver East Provincial Council, but we were in a competitive nomination with Vancouver Centre provincial members, who were supporting Jeff Holter. A woman candidate running for the first time in a macho riding? Could a social worker who was usually an indirect facilitator become an aggressive politician? The group of supporters assured me they would provide lots of help and advice. So I decided to run. I would have a tough fight to win the nomination and to prove that I would be the best candidate for defeating the Liberals.

I was going to have to develop political and campaign skills in a hurry to run in a competitive nomination race. Sandy Bannister, a young aspiring lawyer, chaired our organizing committee. She and many members of Van East NDP began to actively campaign for me. Lil Reid Smith, a mother of six and long-term activist, became my campaign organizer, lining up party members for me to visit and events to attend. Gerry Brown, a creative worker, helped to prepare publicity materials. Bob Williams, a former alderman and by then an MLA, was influential in Vancouver East. He accompanied me on visits to older members, especially those in the Italian community with whom we usually enjoyed a glass of delicious homemade wine.

Lil persuaded Harold Winch, who had been Vancouver East's MP for many years, to write a letter of support for me for the nomination meeting. Harold also critiqued my speeches. He concluded, "Margaret, never be humble. I have never been humble in my life." This may have been helpful political advice, but I began to realize that this personality trait was hard to overcome.

My competition for the federal nomination was Jeff Holter, a labour organizer who had moved into the riding. He was president of Vancouver Centre provincial riding, and a long-time party member. Jeff was also on the Federal Council, and well known to the party establishment from the Barrett-Berger leadership fight. (This did not endear him to Barrett supporters in Vancouver East.) Our campaign support was divided between the two provincial ridings—Vancouver East for me, and Vancouver Centre for Jeff.

Local MLAs were also divided in their support. Norm Levi and Bob Williams supported me, and Dave Barrett quietly phoned key members. Rosemary Brown refrained, claiming I was weak on foreign policy. MLAs Emory Barnes and Gary Lauk also remained neutral.

The competition and tensions peaked as we neared the nomination meeting, which had been called for November 21, 1976. I was surprised and hurt by some of the rumours that were being spread by Jeff's supporters. One was that I was using my position as Manager of the Community Resources Board to refuse social assistance to people unless they signed up to support me. (I had been very pleased when several leaders in public housing wanted to join our campaign). And a quota was imposed to limit the special $1.00 party memberships (previously made available to poor people). I considered this to be discriminatory against poor people and also against me. These dirty tricks taught me a thick skin was needed in politics, where cynicism often prevailed.

By the night of the nomination, both sides had organized well to ensure lots of supporters would get out to the meeting. Lil made me buy a fancy new dress, and Bob helped me rehearse my speech. Claude worked the crowds, full of enthusiasm. The Vancouver Technical School auditorium was jammed with people. It was a tight race. I was nervous but determined to do my best. . . . I won! Afterward we had a great celebration party.

My nomination speech at the meeting had been less policy-focused than Jeff's, but I made many community references and a strong statement of what we needed in Vancouver East. I developed a six-point platform which I continued to advocate during the election period.

Chief among my concerns were jobs for the 14 percent of Vancouver East citizens who were unemployed. It was a huge number, double the national average, and I was determined to promote our NDP goal of full employment at union rates of pay, including pay equity for women and daycare. I called for federal funds for public works projects, industry incentives, and the development of a Community Development Co-operative, which would enable unemployed workers to create their own jobs and provide essential services in their community. I also advocated for protection and expansion of jobs on the waterfront and protection of workers.

I was also concerned that gains made through the National Housing Act to promote rehabilitation of older homes and alternatives for public housing were being undermined by the Liberals. Their MURB (urban renewal) program gave subsidies to developers rather than to tenants and resulted in the demolition of family homes in Grandview to make way for apartments. I proposed that no citizen should have to face housing costs in excess of 20 percent of their income.

This dilemma was not helped by wage and price controls instituted by the federal government's Anti-Inflation Board. Under this draconian measure, negotiated wages of workers were rolled back while the real estate industry was experiencing runaway profits, and increases in the cost of food continued unabated.

Equal rights and opportunities for women were ongoing concerns of mine, as were the rights of minority groups, people with disabilities, New Canadians, and First Nations people. I saw first-hand the poverty in which many of these people lived in Vancouver East. Equality of opportunity was a human rights issue that required federal action.

In my nomination speech I also committed to carrying on the "long CCF-NDP struggle toward a socialist society in Canada," to "distribute wealth through tax reforms, control financial institutions, promote credit unions and co-operatives, eliminate tax rip-offs and foreign control by big corporations, control land resources and energy for Canadians, and to work for international peace and development." Canada, I concluded, "must have progressive social and economic planning under NDP leadership to beat unemployment and inflation and to achieve equal opportunities for all Canadians."

Taking on the Liberals

It was two long years before Trudeau finally called an election in 1979. Meanwhile, after only three years in office, the provincial NDP had called an election—and lost. Dave Barrett lost his Coquitlam seat, and Bob Williams gave up his provincial seat so Dave could run in Vancouver East. Dave won the by-election and then we were represented by him and Alex Macdonald (there were two MLAs representing the riding). When Bob was appointed as an NDP researcher, rumours abounded that he had been "paid off" to give up his seat. Bob remained very active and in control of the Vancouver East provincial executive, waiting for a chance to run again.

The new Socred Minister of Social Services, Bill Vander Zalm, was determined to close down Vancouver's Community Resource Boards, a very progressive NDP initiative. After I became an NDP candidate, I knew my tenure at the VRB was limited. I put out a challenge to Vander Zalm, saying I would quit my job as manager of the CRB if he would restore the Vancouver Resources Board. He laughed—but we got great publicity. Eventually four managers, including me, who coincidentally had NDP affiliations, were given notice. We combined forces, hired a lawyer, and negotiated six months severance pay—enough for me to finance my pre-election campaign.

Now I was campaigning full-time against incumbent Liberal MP Art Lee. We tried many tactics to make me better known. I started a regular column in the local *Highland Echo* newspaper, where the editor was pro Art Lee. The community papers put out by DERA (Downtown Eastside Residents Association) and SPOTA (Strathcona Property Owners and Tenants Association) gave me excellent coverage in the Downtown and Strathcona neighbourhoods.

I had worked in a bilingual (Chinese and English) milieu in Strathcona and constantly reminded our campaign committee that we needed translations. We used Italian and Chinese papers and often got backlash from redneck constituents for our multiculturalism. My friend from community development days, Shane Simpson, helped to boost my public profile. He interviewed me and our interesting guests about local issues on "Van East Report," a community cable TV show that he produced and hosted.

Lil Reid Smith organized regular door-knocking canvasses for me, accompanied by committee members. My aim was to meet people in every poll. Lil made sure I attended party events in all ridings so I would become better known. Gloria Levi also helped us as an organizer. She produced our first brochure, featuring me with a crowd of ordinary folk against the background of the Port of Vancouver.

I had thought that my nomination win would mean smooth sailing with the NDP members in Vancouver East, but that was not to be. One night, after an evening of canvassing, I went to a committee meeting at Lil's house. When I arrived, I was surprised to find my election committee sitting in a circle, waiting to confront me about a meeting I had had with Colin Gableman, a key Holter supporter. I explained that since he was the chair of the federal election planning committee, I was trying to learn more about how we should be preparing. Expecting co-operation, I was amazed at their suspicion. I was learning that in politics past rivalries are rarely forgotten. I was still a naive newcomer who had to earn acceptance and trust.

Politics was a whole new experience, and it was tough. I was used to working with community groups that were non-partisan and relatively kind to each other. And of course I had a good relationship with most of them, so they gave me a lot of feedback. I realize now that community development principles guided my conduct in political life much as when I was working with community groups. I realized that though I may have been naive and humble, I was not interested in becoming a cynical, cut-throat politician. I still had to prove myself with the experienced NDP members. A lot of people on the committee hadn't been close to my activities in the community the way Claude had been. They didn't realize that I had quite a wide range of experience and support that would in fact be very helpful to the NDP.

Learning the ropes was a good, albeit painful experience. It was part of the toughening that I had to go through to be able to defend myself. If you don't go through that with your party, then you're not able to do so with the opposition or in the community. But, even though I had many ups and downs with my planning committee, there was also very good, solid support. I learned that political campaigning involved targeting of supporters and "working from strength," and that I had to be less naive and more focused.

I decided to be more active and visible on important issues in Vancouver East. Unemployment was a major concern Canada-wide, but especially in Vancouver East. I joined the BC Federation of Labour's "Lobby for Jobs." Claude helped to decorate our van and I handed out fliers in front of the Canada Employment offices.

Tiny Himes, a 300-pound ex-seaman, also helped my relationship with unions. He took me to visit most of the union offices and put me on union mailing lists. He also advised me not to be too upset by the rebuffs from Holter supporters. "Kill them with kindness and they'll come around," he advised. And he was right. Tiny often escorted me to party events, especially when a delicious potluck dinner was included. I enjoyed his loud comments.

The party establishment still saw me as a neophyte and a Bob Williams protégée, but a Chinese banquet helped to convince some that I had the wide community support needed to defeat Art Lee. This non-partisan event was organized by my old SPOTA friends in my honour, and I was very moved. I felt an extended family was giving me support. People began to refer to me as "Margaret Mitchell, friend of the Chinese," and the label stuck.

I also got an endorsement from the Italian Garibaldi Club, whose members included old socialists and communists from Italy. Mario Aiello, a younger member of the club, translated, introduced me around, and accompanied me to Italian dinners. Periodically we did a tour up "the Drive" (Commercial Drive), visiting Italian and Portuguese stores and clubs. We knew it was going to be difficult to gain support in the wider (Liberal) Italian community. It was helpful when Dave Barrett reminded folks at Italian banquets that our government had contributed to the Italian Cultural Centre. I was learning crass politics.

. . .

I was told I should ask the NDP Women's Rights Committee to help in my campaign. This committee of feminists helped to develop women's rights policy and agitated for party reforms both federally and provincially.

Although I supported women's rights and had worked with many low-income women, I had not been active in feminist circles. I assumed the WRC would support a 'sister.' However, I was shocked when they seated me in a circle of hostile questioners and began to confront me with, "Are you a feminist? What is a feminist?" I was so stunned I couldn't answer, and then I sputtered, "I think I am. I have always worked to support women." Obviously I didn't pass the test with some, but several women offered to help me. One member of the group, Margaret Birrell, in particular proved to be a very helpful advisor, especially on the issue of decriminalizing abortion. (I later nominated her for provincial party leader, but she lost to Bob Skelley. She was my campaign manager in 1980.)

Fundraising

It was difficult to keep the troops involved over the long, two-year waiting period. Vancouver East held several unique fundraising events, usually organized by Lil Reid Smith. The first was a 'Bump and Hustle' banquet and dance attended by celebrities Ed Broadbent, Grace MacInnis, Tommy Douglas, Harold Winch, and Dave Barrett. I wore a Victorian costume to this mixed-theme event and got to dance with the leader (a coup over Jeff at the time).

Next Lil invented the 'Bowlathon.' We took over a local bowling alley. NDP members were pressured into signing up donors, and unions were challenged to compete. It was a good fundraiser. I, in turn, proposed a Variety Concert held at the Russian Hall and co-opted various artistic friends to perform. The Irish MC became less articulate as the evening and drinks wore on, but we had fun.

Another event I suggested was later described by Harold Winch as "a disaster." Emma Chalmers, a Tongan friend who had joined the party, frequently offered to put on a Luau for us. We finally agreed and booked the new Italian Centre. Tickets were sold throughout several ridings. Emma arranged for cooks to roast the pig as well as for the entertainers, including a fire-eater.

When the day of the Luau came, the meal was late, the ice cream was melted, and the Tongan entertainers had to be rescued by Claude at the Canada-US border. The musicians were served too many free drinks (my mistake), and the fire-eater dropped his torches. To top it off, a well-known member fell in love with a beautiful dancing partner who turned out to be a cross-dresser.

The next day I rushed over to the Italian Centre. The new kitchen was a mess. The pig had been cooked over an open grill and grease was everywhere. As I worked alone to clean up, I cursed my stupidity for suggesting this event. It was quite a while before we could laugh about it.

Another incident made the Mitchells notorious in party circles. Claude volunteered to provide entertainment at a potluck supper. I was sceptical, having performed with Claude before, but was finally co-opted. Claude brought out his Australian bullwhips, positioned me with a lighted cigarette in my mouth, and proceeded with his circus act. The noise echoed in the community centre arena as he came closer and closer with dramatic cracks of the two whips. Finally, he knocked the ash off my cigarette to great applause. Although I became famous for my bravery, I realized this was hardly an appropriate activity for a feminist.

Local Riding Issues

Long before I became a politician, I was concerned about the issues confronting people in Vancouver East—unemployment, poverty, the need for affordable housing, the high cost of living, and the inequalities and discrimination that women and ethnic minorities faced. As I talked to individuals and visited organizations, my concerns deepened. I was aware how little the Liberal government was doing to help people in need and how little Prime Minister Pierre Trudeau cared. I was becoming angry and determined to be a fierce advocate for change.

I talked with longshoremen and other maritime workers about waterfront issues and the need to promote Canadian shipping. Jack Allen, a longshoreman and President of the Adanac Housing Co-op (next door to where we lived), continued to be a very helpful resource person and later became my official agent. As well as criticizing Art Lee and his government, I tried to propose positive solutions that could help my neighbours.

Political Icons

One of the things I liked about the NDP was the way they honoured and respected party elders. I appreciated the advice and friendship of several elders who were founders of the CCF and political icons in our party. They were passionate believers in social justice, and unashamed idealists who were without the cynicism that is common today. In the days before TV, they were outstanding orators and advocates for change.

I had respected and admired Grace MacInnis long before she decided to run for office. She was the daughter of J.S. Woodsworth, the founder of the CCF, which later became the NDP. Grace succeeded her husband as MP for Vancouver-Kingsway. We worked together with poverty groups, and I helped her to set up a Lucy L. Woodsworth Fund for children in honour of her mother. In the early '70s she was the sole female MP in the Canadian Parliament, and when male MPs insulted and patronized her, she called them "MCPs" (male chauvinist pigs).

In the days before feminism, Grace was a strong advocate for family planning and the decriminalization of abortion. She felt mothers should have an income to enable them to stay home to nurture their children. I remember once I attended a poor people's conference in Squamish with Grace. When the group went to the local pub, glasses of beer overflowed our table—I was amazed. They were gifts from miners who had recognized Grace.

Although Grace did not take sides during my fight for the Van East nomination, I know she was pleased when I won. Over the years I often went to her for advice. When she became crippled with arthritis, Claude and I visited her to help with practical things.

I will never forget the passionate speech Grace made in Winnipeg at her last party convention when she introduced Tommy Douglas. We were very low in the polls and members were feeling discouraged at our losses. Crippled with arthritis, she and Tommy, who was dying of cancer, were wheeled through the crowd to the podium. Grace introduced Tommy most eloquently. He brought tears to my eyes when he implored us to never give up the fight for a New Jerusalem. Hundreds of delegates went home inspired to continue the struggle for justice in Canada.

After she died, I presented a eulogy for Grace in Parliament and spoke at her memorial, where Harold Winch moved us with his oratory. (Later I eulogized Harold too.)

Harold Winch became my friend and was persuaded by Lil to provide a letter of support for my nomination. He had been an early founder of the CCF, along with his father, Ernie Winch, and, during the Depression, had once quelled a riot in downtown Vancouver. Harold became leader of the BC CCF in the provincial legislature, and he almost became premier. In 1952 he won the most votes, but the results of the preferential ballot gave the election to the right-wing coalition that became the Social Credit Party under W.A.C. Bennett. Bitterly disappointed, Harold left BC politics and won a federal seat. He represented Vancouver East in the days when there were no flights home, Parliament sat long hours, and alcohol over-consumption was a hazard.

Tommy Douglas, the famous founder of Medicare in Saskatchewan, has remained an icon for most New Democrats. He became the first leader of the newly formed NDP. Perhaps his finest hour was when he stood alone in Parliament to oppose the War Measures Act, imposed by Prime Minister Trudeau in 1970. Many innocent Quebeckers were jailed without trial under this repressive act. Tommy's fame has stood the test of time. In November 2004 he was voted "the Greatest Canadian" in a hugely popular contest on CBC-TV.

Stanley Knowles, who represented Winnipeg for many years, was famous for his fight to win old-age pensions for Canadians. He also was an expert in parliamentary procedure and was respected by all parties. He was my House Leader and friend.

The stories and struggles of these early socialists who were the founders of our party always moved and inspired me. Maggie Black (mother-in-law of MP Dawn Black) was another militant socialist in Vancouver East. Back in the 1930s in Regina, she had helped to feed unemployed workers who were part of the On-to-Ottawa Trek, as they marched to Ottawa to demand help. She married George Black, one of the leaders of the protest, who was jailed and accused of treason. Years later in Vancouver, she continued to organize and to take part in workers' struggles. Maggie always helped in my campaign, keeping records with her friend Olga, and continued to be my good friend. Her daughter-in-law, Dawn Black, has twice been elected as MP for the riding of New Westminster–Coquitlam.

Lo Po Yin, an elderly SPOTA member, was my special supporter in the Chinese community. As I got to know him I loved his stories of his support for Sun Yat-sen in the 1920s, and his important work during the Japanese invasion of China. He recommended Chinese medicine to me, and told me stories of his loving wife and his concubine. Mr. Lo was in his eighties, and although he spoke in support of me at several NDP meetings, he appointed a younger man, Mr. Mak, to be his lieutenant to help in my campaign.

The Fight Begins

After my nomination, our focus shifted to external matters, in particular to defeating Art Lee. I stepped up canvassing, never missed community events, and wrote many press releases. The *Highland Echo,* which covered most of the riding, was supporting Art Lee. One editorial praised him, predicting he would become a cabinet minister. When the editorial criticized the NDP and Harold Winch's past contribution, Harold came back with all guns blazing. He reminded readers that only the NDP had protested discrimination against Orientals during the '40s. At a time when Liberals had disenfranchised Asian and native people, the NDP had demanded they be given the vote.

Art Lee also won the support of United Native Nations (then called BCANSI), led at that time by Bill Wilson. Angie Dennis, a fiery native woman, teacher and NDP supporter, was livid. She prepared a pamphlet criticizing the Liberal White Paper on Indian Policy, which had been rejected by native people. Taking her two boys with her, she distributed a protest paper in all the bingo halls in the riding, asking players to support the NDP.

In August I was on a panel on the BC-TV "Vancouver Show" with Art Lee and an outspoken journalist, Doug Collins. Both were surprised when I became very assertive, challenging their conservative opinions. Claude was very proud of me because at one point I apparently told Collins, "That's bullshit, Doug."

Art Lee had a distinct advantage in Chinatown, even though he did not speak Cantonese. He was supported by progressives who had taken over the Chinese Benevolent Association. SPOTA people quietly supported me but also liked Art. I learned later that my helper, Mr. Mak, was affiliated with the right-wing Kuomintang. I realized I was caught in the middle of Chinatown politics and I faced a dilemma. Dave Barrett advised me to praise Sun Yat-sen, the father of the Chinese Revolution, and both sides would approve.

When I was invited by NDP supporters to visit the Sikh temple I took off my shoes as is the custom, covered my head with a scarf and knelt before the altar. I made a contribution to the temple and joined the men's side. Later I spoke to the gathering along with other candidates. Afterward we enjoyed a meal which the men served in the basement of the temple. NDP supporters in the Sikh community also held a fundraiser for us during each election.

First Election Campaign

Trudeau finally finished a five-year term and called an election for May 22, 1979. The competition heightened as Election Day came near. In 1974 the NDP in Vancouver East had been defeated by only 57 votes and we were determined to win this time. Ed Vassenar, who had been an NDP organizer in Ontario, agreed to manage my campaign and the BC Government Employees Union (BCGEU) gave him leave. The provincial election campaign overlapped the federal for four weeks. During this period, Kingsway candidate Ian Waddell and I shadowed Dave Barrett wherever possible for photo ops. It began to look like he had three heads as we each peered over a shoulder.

As the federal campaign opened, I warned of the threat of spills from dangerous goods in Vancouver East and inadequate fireboat protection. High interest rates, high inflation and high unemployment were blamed on Liberal policies. I was furious when Trudeau came to town and blamed high unemployment on the unemployed. I demanded he apologize, and said, "Instead of telling people to 'get off their asses and get back to work' you should visit the Hastings Canada Employment Centre where thousands of people are applying for work and there are no jobs."

In 1979 the NDP gave major priority to recruiting and nominating women candidates. The aggressive, dedicated women's movement within the party had advanced a Women's Rights policy and women's participation in all levels of the party. I wrote an article for the NDP newspaper, *The Democrat*, detailing our policy and the feminist record of the federal NDP. Our election slogan on T-shirts was "A woman's place is in the House of Commons." (Although more women than ever before were nominated by the NDP in 1979, only Pauline Jewett and myself were elected as MPs. We became close friends.)

After a tightly organized E Day campaign with hundreds of workers "pulling the vote," we anxiously awaited results. A jubilant party began when we learned I had defeated Art Lee by 1,366 ballots, polling 13,557 votes.

CHAPTER 11

Off to Ottawa: The Joe Clark Era

After the May 1979 election and a brief holiday with Claude, I began my life as a Member of the 31st Parliament. In all, Ed Broadbent's NDP had won 26 seats in the House of Commons. Trudeau's Liberals went down to defeat, and Joe Clark's Conservative government was in a minority position. In BC, the NDP increased federal representation from two to eight members—a vibrant, energetic, fun-loving west coast caucus that included Svend Robinson, Ian Waddell, Pauline Jewett, Ray Skelly, Jim Fulton, Sid Parker, Mark Rose, and me. With the election of Nelson Riis, Lyle Kristiansen, Jim Manley and Ted Miller in 1980, the number of BC NDP members rose to 12, but still included only two women. I greatly enjoyed my pals in the BC Caucus and the BC humour of Marc Rose, Ray Skelly, and Jim Fulton, who called me Maggie. We bonded as a family.

I hired Lil Reid Smith, who had been an indomitable organizer and knew everyone in Vancouver East, as my riding assistant. We decided to rent a duplex next to the MLA office as my constituency office. We scrounged furniture, and I invited community groups to use this homey office. Later in September when we held an official opening, Lo Po Yin and Grace MacInnis, two respected elders, were guest speakers.

I convinced my supporters that it was essential to have a Chinese-speaking worker. Nancy Wong was hired part-time and she opened a Saturday office rent-free in the Royal Bank's community storefront branch in Strathcona. I committed to a bi-monthly column for local papers and we continued the "Van East Report" on TV. Later I hosted a reception at Britannia Centre for new immigrants in Vancouver East.

Ed Broadbent, our national leader, called our first caucus meeting, a two-day training session at a resort outside Ottawa. I arrived jet-lagged with a debilitating migraine, which was to become my chronic condition over several years. For some reason, in this new situation, with many experienced colleagues and staff, I regressed to silence in meetings. I felt intimidated by Ed, despite the fact that our BC Caucus had strongly opposed his pro-NATO stance.

Immigration Critic

In 1979 Ed assigned me the role of Immigration Critic. This was to be an active file, since Vietnamese Boat People were posing a massive humanitarian refugee problem. I hired capable Patty Wudel to be my assistant (along with Cathy Prince and Joe Barrett) and she soon had me working on high-profile immigration cases. She proposed I go to the UN Refugee Conference in Geneva with the Canadian government delegation, headed by Immigration Minister Flora MacDonald. Ed agreed this was a good move, and since I was not a government delegate, I paid my own expenses. It was an educational experience to learn the international aspects of this refugee crisis and how the UN worked.

• • •

I returned to advocate that Canada take a larger quota of refugees and that settlement programs be expanded to include help with language training and jobs. I soon learned that many Vancouver East constituents who opposed immigration did not agree with me. It was understandable that families experiencing unemployment would find newcomers a threat, even though immigration created economic stimulus and employment in the long run. I learned to always advocate for jobs and housing for Canadians ahead of refugees. Later I criticized Immigration Minister Ron Atkey for restricting family reunification. This policy meant that many of my constituents would not see family members for years.

Harold Winch, who knew the riding well, sent a message to Ed: "If you want to lose Vancouver East, keep Margaret in Immigration. It is a no winner." Next time Ed made me Housing Critic.

Parliament Opens

After months of preparation and several boo-boos (such as proposing that the Canadian Embassy in Israel be moved to Jerusalem), Joe Clark finally opened the 31st Parliament in the fall of 1979. I was awed by the history and tradition of the beautiful Parliament buildings. I remember walking past the circular fountain embracing the Centennial Flame (also known as the Eternal Flame), up the walkway to the impressive and historic Centre Block, home of the House of Commons. Newly elected Burnaby NDP MP Svend Robinson joined me. Svend, who usually was full of confidence, also was humbled. "Can you believe that we are finally here, Margaret?" he asked. It was a moving moment as we realized how fortunate we were to be there, and how proud we were to be representing Canadians in Parliament.

Parliament was opened by Governor General Romeo LeBlanc, who, following British tradition, read the Throne Speech in the "Upper House," the Senate. We "commoners" were made to stand outside the Senate to listen. Then, following ancient traditions, we dutifully followed the (Usher of the) Black Rod who, dressed in his sombre attire, led us into the House of Commons. . . .

• • •

As the minority opposition party, NDP members occupied the smallest space and were allowed fewer questions in Question Period. However, we were well prepared and Ed always led off forcefully. We criticized the Throne Speech for its silence on unemployment and inflation and the Tory threat to privatize Petro-Can. Mortgage rates were up to 14 percent and there was a national housing crisis. Since Pauline and I were the only two women in caucus, we were assigned seats near Ed in order to be seen on TV. I tried to wear bright colours for the cameras as a contrast to all the men in dark suits—at least we females had this one advantage.

During the first few weeks, new members were given priority to make "maiden speeches" in response to the Speech from the Throne. It was customary to concentrate on constituency issues and to praise our wonderful riding. I had no trouble praising Vancouver East people and challenging the government to deal with our urgent unemployment and housing problems.

I also congratulated the nine women Members of Parliament "who worked twice as hard as our male colleagues to be nominated and elected." As the NDP Immigration Critic, I spoke to the need for a more just and fair immigration policy, and the need for more funding for settlement services. Finally I spoke strongly on the need for an effective Canadian merchant marine, and presented Ed Broadbent's plan of action to rebuild this service. (Several of my close labour friends in the riding had been in the merchant marine during the war and they convinced me that this should be a priority for Vancouver East.)

Since it was 9 p.m. when I rose to speak, the House was almost empty. I was grateful that one sympathetic Tory, David Kilgour, sat through it all and sent me a note of congratulations! (He later became a Liberal and then sat as an Independent.)

Claude continued to be very supportive on the home front, meeting me at the airport each Friday night when I arrived jet-lagged at midnight Ottawa time, often taking me to a meeting at 9 p.m. Vancouver time. He refused to come to "blizzardly cold Ottawa" except when I needed him to help me move. I stayed with my Red Cross friend Pam, and Dick MacLeod, for the first few weeks until I found a one-room apartment near the Hill. My migraine headaches with accompanying vomiting continued for several years. Eventually a chiropractor cured me with neck adjustments.

I did manage to persuade Claude to come to Ottawa for the Governor General's Ball—a glamorous event held at the beginning of each new Parliament. As we lined up to enter Government House we happened to be behind Pierre Trudeau, who was now an ordinary MP in opposition. Claude immediately told him how much he admired him, especially for the way he handled the young "punk" in Alberta (Pierre had grabbed him and lifted him off the ground by his belt—a favourite trick Claude had used in his merry-go-round days). Pierre looked coy and suavely thanked Claude. However, he was deflated when Claude said, "Yes, I admired you—but I would never vote for you."

Claude also took advantage of his visit to attend the Spouses' Tea hosted by Maureen McTeer, the wife of the Prime Minister. As the only male spouse (or "spout" as he called himself) he was in his glory. This partly compensated for not being allowed to deliver me to Parliament on his motorcycle.

Every morning our caucus executive met to select and assign statements and questions for Question Period, held at 2 p.m. Debates on bills and speeches took place later in the day and usually were attended by only a few who were on duty from each party. NDP speakers were limited by the size of our caucus, so there was usually a competition to be chosen by the executive to speak. My staff and I prepared and researched questions, and I occasionally won a place on the agenda.

On October17, 1979, I criticized the Minister of Employment for restricting Employment Insurance benefits for part-time workers, most of whom were women. In my supplementary question I pointed out the double discrimination that immigrant women face and I asked him to extend orientation, language training, and childcare allowances.

I also spoke on the Bill to amend the Old Age Security Act, pointing out the needs of dependant spouses for adequate pension coverage, and recommending pay and pensions for homemakers. "This bill treats a woman as an aging sex symbol rather than treating her with dignity as an independent person with rights in her own name," I argued. I advocated for a social insurance system similar to BC Mincome for all unemployed persons over the age of 60. "Let us plan to set up a Guaranteed Income System to replace our obsolete welfare system by 1995."

On October 18th, the fiftieth anniversary of the Persons Case, I asked the Prime Minister to recognize Grace MacInnis (who had received the Governor General's Persons Award and who was in the gallery) by extending funding for the Anti-Poverty Organization, which she had helped to found. The PM was gracious to both Grace and myself, but, as usual, the government was non-committal in response to my requests.

Daycare on The Hill

My request to the Minister of Health and Welfare to celebrate the International Day of the Child by establishing a model childcare centre on the Hill was received favourably by Minister David Crombie, who was more positive and progressive than most Tories. As a result of this question, several workers on the Hill who had young children came to my office to ask our help in getting a childcare centre started. My staff and I continued to work with them to plan strategies. They signed up other parents to show the need. When Jeanne Sauvé became Speaker of the House, she took up the cause and found a location (despite protests by Senators who said children playing would be too noisy). I was pleased when the centre finally was operational, even though the Liberals took all the credit.

The Late Show

The 10 p.m. "Late Show" was a chance for a Member to elaborate on or challenge some measures that had been raised in the House. At that hour the House usually was empty, but we got our points in the record and could mail copies of *Hansard* out to supporters. I took advantage of this opportunity whenever I could and used it to improve my speaking skills. I spoke on the needs of disabled persons for tax credits, jobs, and accessible transportation. I also pointed out that the House of Commons should be more accessible. (Some time later I noticed seats in the gallery were removed to accommodate wheelchairs.)

The Transportation of Dangerous Goods Act gave me an opportunity to deplore recent chemical spills in Vancouver East and the explosive situation in the Port of Vancouver, where many dangerous modes of transport converge. I called for tighter controls on transportation of dangerous goods.

. . .

The Vancouver housing crisis was worsening. I used the discussion of Bill C20 ("To provide tax credits for mortgage interest and property taxes") to draw attention to the dire situation in Vancouver. I called for the expansion of social housing programs rather than the phoney tax credit gimmick proposed by the Tories, and pointed to the need to reduce monthly payments for social housing to below 20 percent of income.

A Private Member's Bill to amend the criminal code to restrict access to abortions prompted a very emotional response from me. I tried to make each male Member feel what his daughter would face if she had an unwanted pregnancy. I pointed out that abortions by backroom butchers would increase if this bill passed. I talked about the need for children to be wanted and loved and the increase in child abuse when this was not the case. I stressed the right of a woman to make her own decision concerning abortion. The only points raised by a Tory responder were that I had equated vasectomy with abortion and male Members of Parliament were "deeply concerned."

Arrival at the House of Commons in 1980.

Head tax payer Yuen Bok Yee. I initiated the campaign in Parliament to redress Canada's past racist Chinese Head Tax.

At the Poverty Forum with the BC Federation of Labour's Joy Langan, and Bishop Remi De Roo.

Our NDP leader, Ed Broadbent, and I visit with Grace MacInnis, former MP and my mentor.

With former CCF leader Tommy Douglas (left) and NDP House Leader Stanley Knowles.

Discussing the need for social housing with DERA leader Jim Green, Bruce Erickson, and Libby Davies.

Beating Barrett at bocci. With former premier Dave Barrett, Senator Ray Perrault, and Garibaldi Club reps at Italian Market Day.

Vancouver peace rallies were attended by thousands. At this one, Frank
Kennedy of the Vancouver and District Labour Council was MC.

International Women's Day rally.
The women's movement was strong in the 1980s.

With Premier Mike
Harcourt at our annual
NDP fundraiser, a
Chinese banquet at the
Pink Pearl Restaurant.

MLA Bob Williams, here with volunteer Eric Kolle,
helps present recognition pins to community volunteers.

With MP Audrey
McLaughlin, newly
elected NDP leader—a
first for women in
Canada—at the BC
Legislature.

NDP sisterhood in Ottawa: Dawn Black (MP), Rosemary Brown (former
MLA), Audrey McLaughlin (MP), Lynn Hunter (MP), Joy Langan (MP),
Marian Dewar (MP), Pauline Jewett (MP), and Margaret Mitchell (MP).

Ed and Lucille Broadbent join me to help campaign.

My final speech in this Parliament was on the proposed Committee on Volunteerism. I used my time to challenge the traditional concepts of middle-class volunteerism, which featured "ladies bountiful." I praised the many examples of self-help in low-income communities and advocated start-up funding for community development corporations.

Parliament Closes

I was sitting in the House signing hundreds of Christmas cards when the final vote on the Conservative budget was pending. Although we knew it would be tight for the Tories, we expected Joe Clark would persuade the six Quebec Creditiste Members to support him. A sick Tory was brought in from hospital to vote, but Joe must have forgotten to recall Flora MacDonald from Europe. Imagine our astonishment when the Creditistes voted against Joe and he lost! This meant the defeat of the government. After less than a year we were into another election. I rushed home to phone Claude.

CHAPTER 12

Trudeau Returns: Our New NDP Caucus

Trudeau led the Liberals to victory in 1980. In Vancouver East, the election campaign had once more been a battle against Liberal Art Lee. I also faced a Conservative and the usual three Communist candidates who argued against each other. Margaret Birrell was an excellent campaign manager, and hundreds of volunteers helped. I was feeling much more confident in my role as a politician and enjoyed campaigning because it brought me in touch with so many Vancouver East people. We won this election by a slightly larger mandate—just enough to persuade Art to give up politics.

In our new and slightly larger caucus I was appointed Housing Critic. Shane Simpson, an NDP activist from Van East who had grown up in public housing, replaced Joe Barrett as my housing researcher. He stayed two years. Lil Reid Smith continued as "boss" of the riding office (and of me), and Cathryn Prince carried on as my office co-ordinator. She was also my wonderful "care-giver" in Ottawa whom I relied on to keep me on schedule and looking decent. We worked as a collective, and both Lil and Cathryn stayed with me for fourteen years. Patty Wudel was seduced away by our friend Dave McTaggart from Greenpeace and was replaced by Chris Chilton, a former Ottawa alderman. Tommy Tao became my Chinese-speaking staffer part-time in the riding.

It was a tough work and travel schedule for western MPs. The House sat until 10 p.m. most days. By the time Friday came, I crawled onto the plane exhausted and sank into the music of Pavarotti for comfort. Claude always met me, but there wasn't much time at home. Lil had lots of Saturday appointments for me. I used my old social work skills for case work and enjoyed community events. I loved the diversity and community activism of Van East. In many ways my work as an MP was an extension of my community development role. I was an advocate for reforms and continued to help constituents to organize for change.

Fortunately, Claude's years as a bachelor had trained him for self-reliance on the home front. He cooked, laundered, and even sewed. He was proud of me and never hesitated to tell people. We talked on the phone each day. I couldn't have been an MP without Claude's support and practical help. But I was often lonely in Ottawa.

Being an MP was a more than full-time job, with little time for private life. Although I enjoyed the challenges and fun, I often resented the growing public criticisms of politicians as lazy louts who were only out for themselves. I had found most of my colleagues from all parties to be hard-working and sincere, although some with a craving for power had large egos. New Democrats were principled and followed NDP policy—with Ed as our model. I refused to bow to political expediency and became known for my integrity.

Becoming known is essential if an MP is to be re-elected, and publicity is necessary for that to happen. While I was well known in Vancouver East, I had little notoriety in Ottawa (until I spoke out on wife battering). My changing critic assignments was part of the problem, since we were advised to specialize in order to become known. The other part of the problem was the reluctance on the part of the media to see women Members and the issues they espoused as newsworthy. However, I enjoyed a broad interest in social policy, and did what I could to garner attention for social issues and for myself.

By 1982 I was learning to compete in caucus in order to be on the daily parliamentary agenda. I began to shorten and sharpen my questions. I was not an orator and I relied on notes. However, my greatest problem remained getting my concerns before the public. I wondered if this was because of my style, or because the media had grown used to responding to "hard" economic issues raised by macho men, while ignoring "soft" social policy issues raised by seemingly invisible female Members. And

I, unlike many colleagues, was shy about approaching reporters. It was a vicious circle of non-communication.

Ed Broadbent is a likeable, intelligent person with a good sense of humour. Unlike the aggressive BC politicians I knew, Ed had an easy-going style. He created a positive, co-operative caucus, but he relied on his staff for personal support and advice, and sometimes we felt left out. One of Ed's objectives was to focus NDP policy on economic issues, concentrating on employment, tax, and interest-rate policies rather than on social policy, the traditional NDP priority. As a result, those of us with a social policy interest and critic area had lower priority for questions. I grew to resent this. I also felt that I was being ignored as a woman MP who was not as aggressive as Pauline.

Later, Ed's focus on women's issues and social policy in general changed as he was influenced by feminist staff advisors. I also learned to be more aggressive. In 1984, the last time Ed ran as party leader, we had the greatest electoral success of our history, and were doing fairly well in Quebec, where Ed had been hoping to make gains. He got good media attention, and by and large it was a productive period.

Parliament was different with Pierre Trudeau as Liberal leader and Prime Minister. In sharp contrast to bumbling Joe Clark, Trudeau was a sophisticated and sometimes witty PM. But he had lost some of the charisma and glamour of the Trudeaumania years, and he sometimes seemed bored with it all. However, he was still competitive and determined to win every debate. He challenged the media.

I had several run-ins with Trudeau, whose arrogance annoyed me. He was patronizing to women questioners. I objected when he referred to me as "the Honourable Lady" and I insisted that I be called an "Honourable Member," the same as male members.

Trudeau despised westerners because we elected few Liberals and criticized his policies. (Premier Vander Zalm's objection to French on corn flakes boxes may have contributed to his disdain.) One weekend when Trudeau was scheduled to visit BC, he was reported to be ill. When I learned that he had been in New York on a date with Barbra Streisand, I couldn't resist referring to this in my question. "Will the PM apologize for discoing with Barbra in New York last weekend rather than fulfilling his responsibility to deal with unemployment in BC?" He was furious.

I always thought that Trudeau's attraction to young women was adolescent, but his later devotion to his three sons was admirable. Trudeau's earlier reputation as a defender of a "Just Society" had been permanently marred by his imposition of the War Measures Act in 1970 following the FLQ crisis in Quebec. Hundreds of innocent citizens were jailed without trial as a result. By 1982, Pierre and the Liberal Party had lost considerable respect and popularity in Quebec.

While I was social policy critic, my questions were often directed to Marc Lalonde, one of Trudeau's most senior ministers, who had had long experience as a public servant. He was urbane and intelligent and exuded French charm. After one unsatisfactory answer from Lalonde, who was then Minister of Health and Welfare, I tried to get media attention and responded with a Claude expletive, "That's BS." There was uproar over my unparliamentary language and a call for an apology or expulsion from the House. However, I was upstaged by the charming Lalonde, who said graciously, "It's all right, Mr. Speaker, I know the Honourable Member was referring to 'Benevolent Socialism' in her remarks." The next day my nephew, David Speers, who was visiting, presented me with a red T-shirt with "BS" inscribed on the front, and "Benevolent Socialist" on the back. I kept this souvenir for years.

By 1982 the Cold War was at a peak and I joined protests against cruise missile testing in Canada. That spring I was a Canadian delegate to the UN in New York. This was another excellent way to learn more about international issues and UN operations.

Back in British Columbia, Bob Williams and his followers finally decided to challenge Alex Macdonald over the nomination for the second of the two MLA positions. I decided to support Bob because he was a native of Vancouver East and had a long history in the Van East NDP. When I phoned Dave Barrett from Ottawa to tell him, he was furious, arguing, "You don't go up against an incumbent." I held my ground, despite his blast. In my naive but honest approach to politics, I refused to go behind people's backs. Bob lost the nomination to Alex, and I lost rapport with both Dave and Alex.

Work in the Riding

1982 was an active time for me in Van East. I loved the colourful ethnic events. I celebrated Chinese New Year by attending several banquets and the annual Chinatown parade. (Bill Yee, Chinese Benevolent Society president, now gave me lots of recognition.) At the lively Italian Market Day I beat Dave Barrett at bocci. On July 1, I visited six celebrations, including a special citizenship court. In August I spoke at the Japanese Powell Street Festival and attended the opening of a new Sikh temple in my riding.

I also visited local high schools and presented Citizenship Awards (scholarships) each year at spring graduations. I had established a fund for these awards from the generous salary increase that Members of Parliament had voted for themselves. I had opposed the increase, since my constituents were suffering from high unemployment and poverty, so I used this 'tainted' money for high-school awards. Notre Dame High School refused it because of my stand on abortion.

I always found November 11, Armistice Day, to be very emotional. After presenting wreaths at the Grandview Cenotaph, we VIPs marched up "the Drive" to review the troops outside the Legion. Scouts, Guides, and aging Canadian veterans were joined by Italian veterans. Vancouver Alderman Harry Rankin, who had served in Italy, always said jokingly, "What the hell is the enemy doing here?" We all joined in the celebration at the Grandview Legion and I got my usual quota of beery kisses—some from fellow Korean vets.

Unemployment was still a major concern in Van East, and I was frustrated that I could do nothing about it. In 1983 I decided to focus attention on the issue by calling a day-long community meeting. We planned it carefully, inviting constituents and resource people to the Aboriginal Friendship Centre. Bishop Remi de Roo, who often spoke out on the injustices of poverty, and Joy Langan from the BC Federation of Labour were keynote speakers. Despite would-be anarchists who tried to disrupt the meeting, we ended with positive recommendations and a feeling of solidarity.

When the provincial Social Credit government brought in the brutal "Bennett budget" with its drastic cuts to social programs, I was pleased that the Solidarity Movement, formed of unions, community groups, churches, and the NDP, launched a massive protest. I attended, and I also spoke at the End the Arms Rally.

Riding work continued to be my priority. I established a firm policy with staff. My stance was, "Constituents must come first. We must make ourselves accessible to them. If we can't solve a difficult problem, then at least do something to show we care." Many of those problems were immigration problems. Lil became a tough advocate with bureaucrats, and together we managed to solve many difficult cases.

My old and new friends in community organizations kept me informed and asked me to intervene when there were problems. I had a close relationship with ethnic groups. When SUCCESS (an agency serving Chinese immigrants) started a campaign to oppose racism that was expressed in the CTV program "W5," I raised this issue in Parliament. I worked closely with MOSAIC (a multilingual non-profit organization that helps immigrants and refugees settle into Canadian society) too, and was always invited to Chinese library events.

I was frequently invited to open houses and special events held by various local organizations. Some—like Britannia Centre, SUCCESS, and Hastings Sunrise Action Council—remained strictly non-partisan, but they always welcomed me warmly to meetings and events. Other organizations, like DERA and Adanac Co-op, were openly supportive. DERA plastered their office building with my campaign signs.

I also had a network of supporters in the many co-op housing developments in Vancouver East who were pleased that I advocated strongly for their cause. The Native Housing Association also supported me, and a representative often accompanied me on door-to-door visits to native housing tenants. SPOTA continued to be like a family, keeping me up-to-date on Chinatown news. Bessie Lee and Jonathon Lau of SPOTA were my close friends. This continuing grassroots support meant a great deal to me.

My good friend Patsy George, who lived in Grandview, often accompanied me to meetings and events and was always there when I needed her. When Claude refused to go to one of her formal dinner parties, she delivered a hot dinner to him and won him over. They became good friends.

Lil Reid Smith and I worked very closely with Susan Cathcart, the field worker from Canada Employment who was in charge of Canada Works projects. Canada Works was a federal job-creation program that funded short-term community jobs. We established a Community Advisory Group, chaired by Grandview activist Mary Bosze, with representation from each neighbourhood. They gave priority to those projects that would benefit the community as well as provide jobs. While most were not creating permanent jobs, they at least provided some training and made a positive contribution to the community.

I continued to mail out newsletters and copies of *Hansard* speeches to constituents, and submitted columns and press releases to the community papers. By now constituents were probably filling wastebaskets with "Mitchell missives." The Van East Federal Council was a great support to me. They provided advice, and sometimes criticism. Our Chinese banquet at the Pink Pearl Restaurant became an annual tradition where NDP and community people joined me to raise funds and to celebrate.

On the Waterfront

As MP for Van East I had a major interest in waterfront and port issues, and I developed a close working relationship with maritime unions. Union officials took me on tours of the waterfront, informed me of the abuses by waterfront police, and kept me up-to-date on labour-management issues. I learned a lot about shipbuilding, grain handling, and the transportation of dangerous goods, and raised my concerns in the House. I also opposed City of Vancouver plans to sell the fireboats. I arranged meetings with the Port Manager and local residents to discuss environmental and transportation issues. He became very responsive to our concerns, and this became an annual meeting.

Tiny Himes worked for the Seamen's Union and had been on opposite sides to Jack Allen and Tommy McGrath in early waterfront battles. Despite their differences, they were all very helpful to me. Tommy was a pugnacious fighter for seamen and frequently contacted me to protest injustices. On one occasion the marine workers asked me to speak against the closure of the shipbuilding industry in North Vancouver. I was heaved up onto the back of a high truck by two burly marine workers to make my appeal.

My longshoremen friends arranged for me to speak to union members before the election. They were meeting in a gym, which had a boxing ring. After they gave my Tory opponent a hard time I said to them, "If you guys give me a bad time I'll call on my Aussie husband to defend me." A roar went up, "Put him in the ring! Put him in the ring!" I won their votes.

I had used my community development skills to help organize a Waterfront Coalition so community groups and labour representatives could work together to deal with Vancouver Port Authority and various levels of government. Chaired by Jim Green of DERA, the coalition pressed for protections from port pollution and dangerous goods, opposed freeways, and challenged harbour police tactics. Later, this group was active in stopping a waterfront freeway to the port.

As a result of these many contacts, I frequently raised questions in the House on maritime issues. Our caucus strongly defended collective bargaining rights when strikes or lockouts threatened to stop grain shipments from the Prairies to the port.

CRAB Park

Vancouver's Downtown Eastside residents lived in crowded housing, dingy rooms, or on the street, with no access to the nearby waterfront. They were threatened by plans for port redevelopment and a convention centre, which disregarded the needs of this densely populated neighbourhood of poor people.

As MP for the eastern part of the downtown area, I received frequent letters and requests for help, especially from persistent advocate Don Larson, who worked on his own, flooding politicians with well-researched arguments for community improvements. I supported downtown people when they organized a camp-in and tree-planting event on the vacant land to draw attention to their cause. I contacted Bob Williams, who generously donated a very large fir tree, which he paid to have moved and planted on the prospective park site.

Despite many appeals, the Port Corporation (now known as Vancouver Port Authority) refused to change its plans. Since the proposed park site was located in Vancouver Centre, I contacted Pat Carney, the Conservative MP for that riding. In an all-too-rare example of non-partisan co-operation among MPs, we broke with partisan traditions and went together to lobby the Port Manager. Eventually he made a land deal with the Parks Board, and political pressure plus community persistence won a new waterfront park they named "CRAB Park" (or "Create a Real Accessible Beach Park").

Chinese Head Tax Redress Campaign

Throughout my time as MP for Vancouver East, I was involved in many human rights issues that affected my constituents. The NDP had long supported redress for Japanese-Canadian citizens who, during World War II, were classified as aliens, had property confiscated, and were either sent to camps in the BC Interior or deported. Along with Grace MacInnis and our NDP caucus, I continued to support their struggle for justice and redress.

Before 1982, I was aware of the early discrimination against Chinese-Canadians who had come to Canada first during the Gold Rush and afterwards worked as indentured labourers to build the Canadian Pacific Railway. They were paid starvation wages, and many hundreds died in the dangerous work of opening up Canada from East to West. When their labour was no longer needed for the railway, immigration was curtailed. New Chinese immigrants were forced to pay a head tax to come to Canada, which rose to a high of $500 (the price of a house in those days). The Chinese Head Tax policy was replaced by the racist Chinese Exclusion Act from 1923 to 1947, which prevented families from reuniting, and created a lonely bachelor society in Vancouver's Chinatown. Although Asian-Canadians were not allowed to vote until 1947, many had fought in World War II.

In 1982, after Parliament had passed the Charter of Rights and Freedoms, I was confronted with the injustices of the Chinese Head Tax and the Chinese Exclusion Act by two elderly constituents. First Mr. Mak Dak Leon showed me his receipt for the head tax he had paid to come to Canada many years earlier. He said, "Now we have a Charter of Rights, Mr. Trudeau should apologize for Canada's discrimination against the Chinese. He should repay the $500 I paid in tax, with interest." I agreed with him and said I would bring this matter up in Parliament.

Soon after, another elderly constituent, Mr. Shack Lee, showed me a picture of himself as a teenage immigrant to Canada. His extended family, with great difficulty, had paid the $500 head tax to send him to the "Gold Mountain" to have a better life and to help his family. It took him many years to repay the $500 loan. He lived a very lonely life in Chinatown. When he tried to bring his grandson to Canada, he was prevented by the restrictions of the Chinese Exclusion Act. Mr. Lee wanted the Canadian government to apologize for this unjust discrimination against immigrants from China.

I raised this concern in Parliament repeatedly, asking the government to officially apologize for the unjust and racist Chinese Head Tax, and to compensate survivors. The Liberal Minister of Justice was sympathetic and agreed to look into the matter. However, he did nothing. I felt very frustrated.

Meanwhile, Hansen Lau of the Chinese radio station CJOR took up this cause, and asked people who had paid the head tax to bring copies of their receipts to the station. My office was flooded with over 400 certificates. My staffer, Tommy Tao, worked with me on this issue in co-operation with the Chinese Canadian National Council (CCNC), which had begun a Canada-wide campaign. I raised the issue again in Question Period but the Liberals still refused to take action. Prime Minister Trudeau said there were many historic injustices which could not be redressed.

In Vancouver there was a growing split in the Chinese community over this issue. Most older people acknowledged the early injustices, but some community leaders felt the issue was in the past, and opposed seeking financial compensation. Others wanted the early racism to be recognized and redressed. Many grandchildren of head tax payers were actively working in the CCNC national campaign. Newcomers who had come to Canada during the good years were unaware or indifferent.

I was particularly concerned about the impact that the Chinese Exclusion Act had had on families. Wives were left in poverty in China with no hope of joining their husbands. Several of my friends did not know their fathers until they came to Canada, some already in their twenties. I continued to raise this issue in the House to remind the government of the national disgrace and shame of this racist legislation, which all Canadians must bear. I also thought it was important that school children learn of our racist past in order to prevent future discrimination.

The Liberals eventually refused outright to consider redress. The Conservative government of Brian Mulroney responded to public pressure and eventually compensated Japanese Canadians, but they refused to deal with redress in the case of the Chinese Head Tax. Other ethnic groups began to seek redress for early discrimination.

In 2002, after I had retired, I was asked to speak at a head tax rally on Parliament Hill—the 20th anniversary of government inaction. Many of the original leaders of this movement were there and thanked me for my continuing support. In 2005, a documentary film, "The Shadow of Gold Mountain," told the story on CBC-TV of this long and continuing struggle for redress, which I had initiated in Ottawa.

The demand for head tax redress was raised again in the 2005 federal election. Unlike the Liberals, who refused an apology and compensation, the new Conservative Prime Minister, Stephen Harper, formally apologized and provided token compensation to living head tax payers and their spouses.

CHAPTER 13

Housing Critic

The major concern of Canadians and of parliamentarians in the early '80s was the economy: high inflation caused by high interest rates, increasing unemployment, and the housing crisis that was especially severe in Vancouver East. I had worked closely with people and planners in public housing, co-ops, and non-profit housing for years and had seen the effect of Liberal programs that destroyed affordable older housing in the Grandview and Strathcona neighbourhoods. As NDP Housing Critic, I called repeatedly for more federal funding to assist in the development of affordable units in co-operatives and native housing. In every debate I also pressed the federal government to reduce interest rates so young people could afford a home. I concentrated hard on housing as a right, but was weaker on the economics of it.

In Vancouver East I attended a number of openings of new social housing and co-op projects. My experience as a community development worker with Adanac Housing Co-op was very helpful, and co-op members continued to keep me informed. Homeowners suffering from the poisonous effects of urea formaldehyde insulation (UFI) used my office to organize a strong protest, which eventually won some federal compensation.

NDP Housing Plan

In January 1981 Ed Broadbent and Mike Harcourt (the NDP Mayor of

Vancouver) joined me to tour several housing developments in Vancouver East. We presented the NDP plan to deal with the housing crisis and develop affordable housing. This included: long-range government planning with housing as a top priority; a mortgage assistance plan to reduce interest rates for first-time homeowners; land banking with federal and provincial crown lands and subsidies; a 100-percent capital gains tax on resale of homes; and an emergency meeting of governments, housing organizations and people affected to take co-operative action.

Outreach—Maritimes

In the early '80s I visited housing developments in the Atlantic provinces. Outreach in the Maritimes was especially important since we had no NDP MPs from that region. Through these visits I gained a broader national perspective and a great fondness for Maritimers and the people of Newfoundland-Labrador.

I first went to Newfoundland in 1980. The National Anti-Poverty Organization (NAPO) had asked me to intervene on behalf of Newfoundlanders who were trying to use RRAP (Residential Rental Assistance Program) to fix up their homes, and to get support for the local RRAP program, which needed more federal funds.

Many unemployed Newfoundland fishers lived on the rocky shores of the peninsula. Although very poor, they owned their own homes and could do their own repairs in the off-season. However, CMHC would not approve plans without their conforming to urban standards—including flush toilets (on rock?). I drove up the Northern Peninsula with the mayor of Parsons Pond in his truck. We stopped in several fishing outports and he introduced me around. I was charmed by the locals (who called me "lass") and I strongly advocated for them when I returned to Ottawa. Eventually CMHC adopted more flexible policies and flush toilets were no longer a priority.

In St. John's I was entertained on board ship by Tommy McGrath, my old CBRT (Canadian Brotherhood of Railway and Transport Workers) pal, and also met with women's groups. Then I flew north to remote areas of Labrador to visit the native community near Happy Valley – Goose Bay. They were building prefabricated houses brought in from BC. One elder, who had always been nomadic, had put up his tent inside his cabin to feel more at home. I was introduced to native food and visited their modern health clinic.

On my way back I stopped in Labrador City, where union members introduced me to local miners. Everyone deplored the past giveaway (by Premier Joey Smallwood) of Churchill Falls power. Quebec was making huge profits selling this electricity to New York—while Newfoundlanders starved.

On another trip I toured Nova Scotia, looking at housing and talking to low-income groups. I was joined by two of my constituents who were also housing experts, Nora Curry and Bessie Lee. We were royally entertained by the New Democrats, especially by Alexa McDonough. She would become the federal NDP leader in the late '90s. In New Brunswick our tour ended with a massive feed of lobster—fourteen per person!

In 1982 I was invited to join the Co-op Housing Federation's tour of Workers' Co-operatives in Britain, France and Mondragon, Spain, and Claude went with me. We were impressed with the variety of enterprises that were operating under co-operative management. The most interesting were in Mondragon, where inter-related co-op industries and services provided jobs for everyone and a safety net when needed. Mondragon had developed an independent, self-sufficient, co-operative economy, which had been initiated by a local priest after the Spanish Civil War. I longed for a similar Canadian response to the many difficulties facing my constituents in Van East.

Nigeria

During my 14 years in Parliament, I was privileged to participate in three parliamentary trips to Africa. Usually the guys on the caucus executive managed to assign the trips to themselves, but in 1981, when no one else was interested, I was allowed to go to Nigeria. I was delighted.

In Lagos I attended meetings of the Inter-Parliamentary Union (IPU), where MPs from many countries held consultations. In the evening, from my high-rise hotel, I saw workers carrying huge loads silhouetted against the orange-purple sunset of Africa.

Nigeria is an artificial country formed by Britain from three warring tribes. Now tensions pervaded the air. As we drove to meetings we cringed at the antics of many wild teenagers who shot off guns from the back of trucks. Garbage was everywhere.

After the conference I decided to travel on my own to Kano in the northern desert, where I visited CUSO volunteers. I soon learned how a lone white woman is treated in a Muslim country. Being an MP meant nothing. I was ignored at the hotel, and finally given a room in a back shed. I later moved to an evangelical missionary enclave, where American standards were imposed behind high walls.

CUSO volunteers took me to a huge old market where slaves had once been chained and sold, now kept as a kind of historic site. I bargained for African crafts. As I lined up at the airport to leave, I again experienced discrimination. I was pushed to the end of the line and studiously ignored by the ticket taker when I refused to pay a bribe. Eventually an American man intervened and helped me through a rather frightening experience. Clearly equal rights for women was not a universal concept.

CHAPTER 14

Women's Rights and Social Policy

During the '70s, the NDP Participation of Women Committee (POW), led by determined feminists, became very militant, demanding greater equality for women at every federal convention. They caucused, developed strategies, and organized. As a result, the NDP adopted policies making equal participation of women in party structures ("parity") and active recruitment of women candidates a top priority. In 1975, the POW Committee had developed a strong feminist agenda and endorsed Rosemary Brown to run against Ed Broadbent for leadership of the NDP. Many traditional party members reacted against these "mouthy" feminists. Some older women felt excluded. I supported POW and Rosemary.

Although Rosemary lost by a few votes, this leadership race marked a turning point in the NDP. Ed became a convert and hired a feminist advisor, who also advised caucus members, increasing our consciousness of women's issues and women's rights. The NDP was the only party to make women's rights a priority.

Slowly other political parties began to realize that they must encourage greater participation of women in politics. More women began to run as candidates (although rarely in winnable ridings) but very few were elected. In 1980, out of a total 295 MPs, only 29 were women. By 1989, only 39 Members of Parliament were women. During both of these terms, only six women held Cabinet positions. The NDP had two women MPs in 1980, and five in 1989. This was to remain the size of our Women's Caucus while I was in Parliament.

My experience as a candidate was more positive than that of most women. I was nominated in a winnable riding with the support of a strong party organization. Despite this, some people were prejudiced against a woman candidate until I had proven myself to be a winner and a hard-working MP. (After a long tradition of male representation for Vancouver East, the culture changed following my period as a Member of Parliament. Women MLAs and women MPs followed me. Vancouver – Hastings MLA Joy McPhail, who became Provincial NDP leader, Vancouver – Mount Pleasant MLA Jenny Kwan, and Vancouver East MP Libby Davies all became outstanding representatives for Vancouver East ridings.)

After my nomination I continued to be an advocate for women. Often I was invited to speak to prospective women candidates who asked what it was like in a male-dominated Parliament. I used my satirical poem to explain.

A Woman's Place is in the House

(Dedicated to Women Candidates)

They say that woman's place is not to roam.
"Stick to the pots—stay close to home
Why should you want to run for office?
That's for men to do—to make laws for us."
Others declare, "Of course you should run,"
But shake their heads sadly because you're a mom.
"Who will take care of her poor little tots?"
They whisper, "Kids need their mother a lot."
You must smile very sweetly but firmly declare
That "raising the kids is a job we will share,
Along with cooking and cleaning and such.
We could all use a wife, thanks very much."
You'll doubtless be warned that you're not tough enough—
A lady's refined—just a cute piece of fluff,
And politics being a dirty male game
Your feminine health will not bear the strain.

The campaign is on and you gather support;
You door-knock, do "clips," and work like a sport.
The battle gets dirty but still you hang in—
This is a fight you're determined to win.
Women MPs find they've only begun
When they arrive in the House to join in the fun.
All Members are "he" and their spouses are "she"
And female intruders should pour out the tea.
But times are a-changing and women all vote.
We work for reforms, and battering's no joke!
Our numbers are growing, our power will increase.
Before long, dear Sisters, this world may have—PEACE!"

Women in Parliament

When I arrived in Ottawa in 1979 I was shocked at the male-dominated culture. As I entered the Parliament building, I was usually stopped by security staff, who assumed that since I was a woman that I was a secretary. Washrooms for women were not as available as those for men. The language of documents and parliamentary reports was always masculine. (I strongly opposed this when I was briefly on the Members' Committee in 1987; I was not reappointed.) A general air of male superiority dominated the halls of power.

Fortunately our leader, Ed Broadbent, was a feminist convert, and most of our caucus members were sensitized to women's rights. I was pleased that our NDP Caucus treated Pauline Jewett and me as equals and did not hold doors for us. Male colleagues were quickly chastised by us for any sexist comments and attitudes. I became an active defender of women's rights.

Although I was enjoying Parliament, I found that women MPs had a very restricted social life, and evenings were lonely when the House was not sitting. I visited the McLeods and McLures (former Red Cross pals), and for a time enjoyed having my niece Susan Learoyd as my roommate. My friend Maeve Hancey contacted me for weekend walks when I was in Vancouver. Most Friday nights I flew home for a hectic weekend of riding work, with little time for Claude.

I formed a close friendship with Pauline Jewett, the only other female NDP MP. We supported and complemented each other—she being the experienced intellectual (the former president of Simon Fraser University—where Claude had taken a Women's Studies course) and I being the grassroots "people person."

Pauline was a political "junkie" and an expert on international affairs. She had been a Liberal MP when Lester B. Pearson was Prime Minister, and later joined the NDP. She moved to British Columbia to become the first woman president of a university in Canada. When she decided to seek an NDP nomination in Burnaby, she was defeated by Svend Robinson, but went on to win in New Westminster. All three of us were elected to Parliament in 1979.

In Ottawa, when the guys went to the Press Club to drink and gossip, Pauline and I had dinner in the parliamentary dining room or at our "pads." At caucus retreats we shared a room. Her smoking and drinking went on late into the night. I was kept awake to sing old cowboy songs or to rate the sex appeal of opposition MPs. (My choice of Tory MP John Crosby was never forgotten or forgiven).

Women parliamentarians in our party carried two important roles. In addition to representing constituents and carrying caucus responsibilities, we represented Canadian women and were expected to be role models and advocates for women's rights. I enjoyed the extra responsibilities of meeting with women's groups in Ottawa and across the country. The warmth and support of sisters sustained me; as well it ensured that I reflected a feminist agenda.

I met hundreds of Canadian women when travelling on the NDP Older Women's Task Force, with the Health and Welfare Committee, and with the Special Committee on Childcare. Every year I was actively involved with the National Action Committee (NAC) women when they lobbied parliamentarians. They were also helpful resource persons on women's issues. I continued to advocate for poor women and immigrant women who felt powerless. My relationship with aboriginal women deepened as I supported their fight for "Indian Rights for Indian Women" and for issues of concern to Inuit women. Women lawyers were wonderful resource persons on constitutional issues, as were daycare advocates in our fight for universal childcare.

Social Policy and Status of Women Critic

My growing concern for justice and equality for Canadian women permeated my day-to-day work in Parliament and in my riding. Although I had been involved in women's issues since I was first elected, I was not appointed Critic for Status of Women until 1982, when I replaced Pauline Jewett, who went on to concentrate on Foreign Affairs.

My shift to the critic areas of Social Policy and Status of Women was a good fit, since I found that most social policy issues were also related to women's rights. I raised concerns regarding increasing poverty, the needs of older women, and the need for childcare. I also fought to retain the universal family allowance.

Counteracting Poverty, and the Task Force on Older Women

As a former social worker and resident of Vancouver East, I was aware first hand of the debilitating effects of poverty on thousands of people. Life was particularly hard on single mothers on welfare and for those working for low incomes. I often raised these issues in Parliament, advocating for an adequate guaranteed income with income supplements for the working poor as well as affordable housing, childcare subsidies, and job strategies.

During the hearings of the 1981 Task Force on Older Women we heard many sad stories of loneliness and poverty, inadequate housing, and lack of pensions for homemakers who had given their lives to families. I represented the caucus, chairing hearings held in many locations across Canada. Sessions were not well attended and the media paid little attention, indicating the neglect by society in general of the problems facing older women. The NDP published a well-documented report, but little action followed. In the House of Commons, Winnipeg NDP MP Stanley Knowles and I continued to advocate lowering the age of eligibility for pensions for women and access to the Canada Pension Plan for homemakers.

Caring for Canada's Children

In belated recognition of International Year of the Child, a special study of children's needs was undertaken by the Health and Welfare Committee. I wrote an NDP minority report, which was praised by our leader (kudos at last). We called for a national childcare program, reform of the Child Tax Credit, preventive programs financed by Canada Assistance Plan, and a federal Children's Bureau. In 1987 a Special Committee on Child Care was established by the Conservatives, but after considerable work, no action was undertaken. It wasn't until 1989, when Ed Broadbent was retiring, that there was unanimous consent in Parliament to end child poverty by the year 2000. However, despite this agreement, the rate of poverty continued to escalate across Canada, and the Broadbent resolution was ignored.

CHAPTER 15

No Laughing Matter

An incident in the spring of 1982 brought spousal abuse to the forefront of Parliament and the nation as a whole. Many male Members of Parliament responded callously to my statement that one in ten Canadian women was subjected to spousal abuse. Television cameras captured their outrageous behaviour and my furious response (described in my Preamble). Women's groups across the country mounted a major protest against the appalling attitudes this behaviour expressed, and many individual men and women wrote to their MPs.

While I was working on the joint standing committee on Justice and Health and Welfare, I heard of the suffering many battered women were experiencing, usually in silence, with no safe haven or recourse. Those with children and no source of income were usually trapped, with nowhere to go for safety. Since family violence was considered a private matter, police rarely intervened. As a result, women often blamed themselves and tolerated the abuse. What's more, unfortunately the violent behaviour often ended up being repeated by their children.

There was an urgent need for government action. Government needed to treat domestic violence as a crime, to retrain police officers to intervene in domestic violence, and to fund transition houses for women and children with help for them to find a secure new life. This is what the joint committee had recommended. Eventually both senior levels of government introduced changes in response to those recommendations, and the video footage of that incident in the House became educational material used in workshops on family violence and by television programmers exploring the subject of spousal abuse. For years afterward women confided that my spirited response to the men's ridicule gave them the support they needed to leave an abusive situation. It might very well have been, as one woman put it twenty years later, "a turning point in feminism in Canada." It certainly became my claim to fame.

Equality Issues

The National Action Committee on the Status of Women (NAC) annual conference was an important event when women demanded that each political party respond to their concerns. Our party always took this very seriously. We required caucus members to prepare and to attend the lobbying session, and we raised most of their concerns in Parliament. I also met with the Canadian Day Care Advocacy Coalition, which was becoming a strong voice. Women in both these movements were helpful consultants and advocates.

. . .

When I became the Status of Women Critic in 1982, I hired Hilary McMurray as my researcher. She was bright and aggressive, and, with NDP Researcher Karen Stotsky, we worked in close collaboration with the women's movement (NAC and POW, the NDP Participation of Women Committee) and with the Canadian Labour Congress (CLC).

One pressing area of concern was the feminization of poverty. Most single moms were poor, welfare rates were below poverty lines, and women earned 70 percent of men's wages. I called for affordable childcare, equal pay for work of equal value, and increased welfare rates.

. . .

Computers were beginning to take over offices. We researched the potential impact of micro-technology on women's employment opportunities, and called for protections. I criticized government wage cuts and advocated mandatory affirmative action in the public service and I continued to push for changes to Unemployment Insurance to cover part-time workers, most of whom were women.

Subsidies for childcare, tax credits, and parental leave would have gone a long way to alleviating the financial stress on women and their children, and I called on the Liberal government to initiate such action. I was particularly concerned with the increase in teen pregnancies, and I opposed the cuts to federal funding for Planned Parenthood.

Many immigrant women, particularly those working as nannies, also needed protection. And older women especially needed a helping hand with finding employment, securing affordable housing, and in retirement. I advocated for employment initiatives for older women, better housing conditions, and pension reform that would protect women in their "golden" years.

There was no shortage of issues that affected women but it was difficult to detect concern, much less action, in the Liberal government.

Abortion

I continued to speak in the House in favour of a woman's right to choose, and to advocate for decriminalization of abortion, despite the hate campaigns of REAL Women of Canada and the opposition of the Catholic Church in my riding. At election times, the campaign heated up with anti-choice demonstrations. The local priest counselled against supporting the NDP, but many parishioners voted for me anyway. Grace MacInnis advised me, "Never compromise your principles. People will respect you even if they don't agree with you."

Going to the Supreme Court in Ottawa with fellow NDP MP Svend Robinson to hear Dr. Henry Morgentaler win his case to legalize abortion clinics was a high point in my political career. I rejoiced for women.

Prostitution

Street soliciting was a major problem in Vancouver East. It had moved from the West End to Mount Pleasant and eastward as city bylaws and police restricted soliciting by sex trade workers. Under federal legislation, prostitution was legal but street soliciting was not. Prostitutes were picked up by police, charged and released, but there were no restrictions on pimps or johns.

I was frequently contacted by angry neighbours who wanted me to do something about soliciting near schools, condoms in lanes, and prostitutes on streets. Businesspeople downtown were losing trade and closing stores. I was sympathetic to neighbourhood problems, but also concerned that women who were poor, often abused and addicted, not be victimized. Many prostitutes were teenagers. These women faced serious dangers on the streets, and many disappeared.

Vancouver Mayor Mike Harcourt pressed the federal government to strengthen laws governing prostitution. The NDP pressed for tougher sanctions against customers and pimps and for protection of minors. Some sought decriminalization. Legalizing brothels would take prostitution off the streets. I tended to sympathize with this position provided it did not involve minors.

I met with neighbourhood groups and workers, and paid a midnight visit to a church-run drop-in centre for prostitutes. I also met with representatives from PACE, a group formed by former prostitutes to provide alternatives to the sex trade. I went on a midnight shift of the Hastings Street beat with city police and visited the jail. I also called a special meeting of concerned people who reiterated complaints. None of these efforts resulted in solutions.

Neighbourhood problems continued while downtown women disappeared. The full extent of this tragedy was not made public until 2002 when police finally reported over 60 missing women, and charged Willy Picton with the murder of over 20 of them. I could not comprehend the enormity of this slaughter. Many of these women had been my constituents. Police took no action except to move women from one location to another. This was one of the most frustrating challenges of my time as a Member of Parliament.

Evelyn's Story

Evelyn lived near my community office with her immigrant parents. As a pre-teen she was a pacifist, and was very concerned about war and peace. She often came to my office to express her concerns. I forwarded her very eloquent letter to Prime Minister Trudeau. When the Premier of China visited Vancouver, she asked if I could give him her letter asking him to work for peace. Although it was not protocol, I delivered her letter to the Premier personally at a Chinese banquet. Later a poem Evelyn had written was published in my newsletter in January 1985.

When Evelyn was in her early teens, she came to my office to say she could no longer tolerate living at home where her parents were very strict.

An NDP member who was also a pacifist befriended her, but eventually Evelyn left home. Her life on the streets is described in detail in her book *Runaway*. It provided a rare glimpse into the life so many young people on the streets endure. Now Evelyn (Lau) is a well-known BC writer and poet.

CHAPTER 16

A New Constitution and Charter of Rights

W omen's rights in Canada required a Charter of Rights that would
entrench equality. Pierre Trudeau's primary focus as Prime
Minister in 1980 was to repatriate and amend Canada's Constitution. The
British North America Act of 1867 still resided in the United Kingdom,
and any changes required the sanction of the British Parliament. Canada
had to go through the Queen, so in effect we were still a colony.

Nationalism was growing in Quebec during the late '70s, led by
Premier René Lévesque and the separatist Parti Québécois. In 1980a
provincial referendum on Quebec sovereignty was defeated by a 60
to 40 percent vote. Trudeau, who was a strong federalist, immediately
assigned his Justice Minister, Jean Chrétien, to begin the groundwork
for repatriating and changing the Constitution. This required extensive
consultation with provinces who rarely agreed. The process began in
Parliament, where the NDP played a major role in drafting the Charter
of Human Rights and Freedoms—supporting the government while
negotiating changes. I did ask for the involvement of my constituents via
a letter, particularly to ensure that aboriginal rights and women's rights be
entrenched. However, there was little interest in constitutional matters in
Vancouver East and I received no replies.

The 1982 constitutional proposal guaranteed fundamental Rights
and Freedoms, including freedom of conscience and religion, freedom
of expression and association. "Every individual is equal before and

under the law." It included an amending formula and the principal of equalization, allowing richer provinces to share with poorer ones. Of primary importance to Trudeau was the protection of French and English language rights.

Our party has a strong commitment to human rights, and we were deeply involved in preparing a draft Charter of Rights and Freedoms. Ed Broadbent advocated for changes requested by women's groups and by aboriginals. He consulted with Trudeau, and we helped to add amendments that recognized provincial concerns, entrenched aboriginal rights, entrenched equal rights for women, and recognized our multicultural reality. This draft was taken to the provinces for approval.

Women Gain the Notwithstanding Clause

Agreement was not reached without much internal and external conflict. Saskatchewan Premier Allen Blakeney opposed a Charter of Rights and Freedoms, arguing that Parliament, rather than judges, should decide on rights. I was ashamed that an NDP Premier would be so insensitive to the need to protect aboriginal and women's rights. Blakeney's stand caused a split in our party as well as between provincial premiers. Their compromise was to introduce a Notwithstanding Clause that would allow provinces to override Equality Rights. Canadian feminists were furious and they organized a remarkable rebuttal. I joined them.

. . .

My role was to work with Pauline Jewett and other women to ensure entrenchment of full equality for women. We were all concerned that Section 15, the "equality clause," would still not fully protect women's equality. Doris Anderson, Chair of the Canadian Advisory Council on the Status of Women, resigned after Minister Lloyd Axworthy prohibited women from holding a women's conference on the constitution. Thus began a remarkable feminist revolution led by the "Ad Hoc Committee"— a group of women activists, mostly from Ontario.

While Pauline, who was on the Constitutional Committee of Parliament, worked with the academics and policy makers, I helped women to organize. I assigned Patty Wudel, my assistant, to work full time with the Ad Hoc Committee that was organizing a women's conference. I also turned over my office and phone full time to the Ad Hoc Committee and became a wandering gypsy.

Advised by Marilou McPhedran and other leading women lawyers, the women insisted on stronger protections to prevent provinces from overriding women's rights. After aggressive lobbying, they persuaded the all-male decision-makers to add Section 28 to the Charter to entrench equality—a great achievement that continues to protect women.

I also met with native women about their concerns and disagreed with my friend, Jim Manley, our Indian Affairs critic, who felt that the right to self-government should supersede rights of native women. Earlier I had supported native women who were organizing to restore band membership rights, which the Liberals had denied to women who had married non-Indians. (While they were in town to advocate for the restoration of women's rights, four BC native women shared my one-room apartment. We had a jolly pyjama party before they took on Parliament Hill.)

The "Night of the Long Knives" became infamous in Canadian history. Unable to get Quebec approval for the proposed constitution, provincial premiers took advantage of Premier Lévesque's absence late that evening and voted to approve the amended constitution without him. The process, which was to have counteracted Quebec separation, resulted in the irreparable exclusion of Quebec, creating deep resentments that almost destroyed our country.

Trudeau immediately instructed Jean Chrétien to fly to London with the new Constitution for approval by the British Parliament and the Queen. As part of the Constitution Act, 1982, the Constitution of Canada, with a Canadian Charter of Rights and Freedoms, was signed on April 17th in Ottawa by the Queen and Prime Minister Trudeau. I felt that I was in Parliament at a historic time, and I learned a great deal about constitutional matters. However, while we were engrossed in our Ottawa ivory tower, my constituents showed little interest in the distant and abstract negotiations. Jobs and high rents were more important.

The Trudeau government was defeated in 1984, and after a brief term by John Turner, Brian Mulroney would become our new Prime Minister.

CHAPTER 17

The Mulroney Era

A fter making more than a dozen patronage appointments to the Senate, Trudeau finally decided to step down, and the Liberals elected John Turner as the interim Prime Minister. We began to prepare for the 1984 election. Glen Sandford was my campaign manager-in-training under Margaret Birrell. Our opponent was Jack Volrich, the defeated Mayor of Vancouver, who decided to run in Vancouver East for the Conservatives. The *Vancouver Sun* and *Highland Echo* newspapers took it for granted he would win, but they were wrong. We trounced Volrich, and he came in third.

Poor John Turner. He had been undermined by the legacy of Trudeau's patronage appointments, made in the last days of his reign. Brian Mulroney, the Conservative leader, challenged Turner during the televised leaders' debate to rescind those appointments. The clip on TV showing the self-righteous Mulroney saying "You had a choice, Sir" was repeated throughout the campaign. Mulroney, when elected, went on to exceed the Liberals in the dispersal of patronage.

The change from a Liberal to a Conservative government met with much fanfare and dramatics from Mulroney. He was determined to outshine Trudeau and become the Ronald Reagan of Canada. We hated the aggressive neo-conservative agenda that was being imposed by Margaret Thatcher in the UK and Reagan in the US, and feared for Canada under a Conservative prime minister.

Soon after the election, Mulroney persuaded his friend "Ronnie" to come to Canada on a state visit. Great plans were made for a Canadian reception that included a ceremonial parade to the Parliament Buildings, a speech by President Reagan to the Canadian Parliament, and a gala performance in the evening.

We New Democrats were very opposed to this visit, but we were told we had to behave according to parliamentary protocol. RCMP in full dress lined their horses up on either side of the entrance for the parade. I was not sure if this was to impress the President or to protect him from hostile Canadians. The horses showed which side they were on when the one in front of me let out a great blast of wind as the President passed by.

In the House, we MPs shuffled in to take our seats. Senators were seated in the middle aisle and the galleries were full of excited observers. After Mulroney's flowery introduction, President Reagan rose to speak. And so did our radical protestor, MP Svend Robinson, who despite orders from our leader to be respectful, shouted out his protest and left the House. According to news reports, this became an international incident. Svend was reprimanded for ignoring a caucus decision to behave. As usual, he ignored the reprimand.

The evening gala was held at the National Arts Centre, with many (except New Democrats) in full formal dress. Here Brian was in his glory, on stage with his wife Mila and President and Nancy Reagan. He and Maureen Forrester led the quartet in an exuberant rendition of "When Irish Eyes Are Smiling" to cement Canada-US-Irish solidarity.

Free Trade had been Mulroney's big election issue and he soon started negotiations on the North American Free Trade Association (NAFTA). Meanwhile his hatchet men prepared to cut social programs (which during the election he had called a "sacred trust") and to "downsize" government services.

We were very concerned that the NAFTA would undermine Canadian sovereignty over our resources, communications, and public programs. The effect would be to reduce and privatize our social and health programs to a "level playing field" with the US. Many Canadian jobs would be lost. We continued to join with the labour movement in many anti-NAFTA protests held across the country.

The 33rd Parliament was my busiest and most productive period as an MP. I was more experienced and more confident, and I continued to enjoy politics. In addition to being Critic for Status of Women and Social Policy, I now was assigned responsibility for Health. I was also active as secretary of the Caucus Executive, which met each morning, and I had parliamentary committee responsibilities. As Social Policy Critic I was the NDP Member on the Special Committee on Child Care, which the Conservatives established. This committee spent months travelling across Canada and to the North to hear presentations on the desperate need for a national childcare program.

. . .

In 1985 the Conservatives were preparing to add another layer of cuts to social programs. It felt like we were starting the battle all over again, with pensions and family allowances on the chopping block. I strongly protested the de-indexing of old-age pensions and presented many petitions opposing this, always a few at a time to keep the issue alive. But in the end, it was an old woman from Quebec who forced Mulroney to back off—with her now-famous poke in the chest, which was caught on camera and broadcast on national television.

The well-being of women and children continued to be a priority for me. I challenged the government to reinstate funding for family planning, citing the increase in teen pregnancies. Several times I raised concerns about abuse in families, and the need for more shelters for women and children who were forced to leave their homes because of violence.

I also pressed for a just employment equity policy for women and minorities. I opposed the Conservative program, extolled by Employment Minister Flora McDonald, because there was no enforcement of affirmative action. The Human Rights Commissioner agreed with me that he did not have the resources or power to force compliance.

Nairobi, Kenya—UN Decade of Women Conference

In July 1985 I was a Canadian delegate to the UN Decade of Women conference held in Nairobi, Kenya. The Canadian government delegation to the Nairobi Conference was comprised of representatives of each federal party, provincial ministers, as well as other well-known women. As Status of Women Critic, I represented the NDP. I had known Doris Anderson when she quit her job as President of the Canadian Advisory

Council on the Status of Women, starting the feminist protest, which
gained Equality Rights in our Charter. As their President, she was
representing the National Action Committee on the Status of Women
(NAC) at this conference. I roomed with Diane Wood, the Canadian
Labour Congress representative. We socialist activists quickly bonded,
and shared our frustration at the bureaucratic control of the Canadian
delegation—and also shared a lot of laughs.

It was a fascinating experience joining with women from all over the
world, learning about their problems and achievements, and formulating
resolutions to move us forward in the next millennium. Each country was
asked to present a report. There was a gasp, followed by boos, when the
Canadian Minister Responsible for the Status of Women came forward.
We were very embarrassed because our minister was a man (Walter
McLean). The Conservatives had managed to denigrate months of work
by Canadian women with this insensitive appointment.

The UN process of building consensus and developing language
that is universally acceptable is arduous. The US delegation was isolated
behind tight security, and often vetoed positive policies. Our delegation
was controlled by External Affairs staff, and delegates had no meaningful
role. In protest, Diane Wood and I decided to take over the Canadian
delegate chairs for one session. Since I had no job to do, I got to know
some of the indigenous women from different countries and helped them
to organize a presentation.

Reports revealed the disparity between the lives of women in
developing and industrialized countries. Women from developing
countries struggled with survival issues—desperate poverty, the need
for more food and clean water, for health care and family planning, for
education and paid jobs. African women carry tremendous burdens in
rural communities: feeding families, growing crops, and walking miles
for firewood while men are usually unemployed and absent. Girls rarely
have schooling. Genital mutilation is a common practice in many
countries. Muslim women stayed apart from other delegates and (like
Canadians) had male spokespersons. (The AIDS epidemic, which was to
add intolerable tragedy to the lives of African women, was not yet voiced
as a concern.)

Women from industrialized countries reported continuing poverty and struggles for equality rights, childcare, job opportunities, and pay equity. Abortion rights were controversial, with the US vetoing recommendations on choice. However, despite economic and cultural differences, the common bond of sisterhood between women soon developed.

Kenya wasn't all work and no play. I went on two safaris with new friends Doris Anderson and Diane Wood. At Hilltop Lodge (where Elizabeth became Queen when her father died) we watched all night as wild animals paraded in hierarchical order to the salt bed in front of the glassed observation room. The second safari was by jeep into the Serengeti plains of Tanzania. We drove close and photographed wildebeest, giraffes, zebra, and sleeping lions, which woke up, had sex, and then slept again. I will always remember looking down at the masses of pink flamingos in the Rift Valley when we drove north to a Canadian-backed development project.

Northwest Territories

I was very pleased to be invited to speak to women's groups in Yellowknife in 1986. Northern women were most welcoming, and I learned a lot about the struggles of living in the harsh northern climate. The high cost of living in the North, the isolation, and the weather make life difficult. Transplanted southerners usually stay only a few years. Most jobs are with government. There are no reserves, and First Nations people are represented in Territorial government.

I stayed with my friend Toni Graeme and her partner in her log cabin outside the town. We carried a toilet bag to the dump each day. It was fascinating to see how northern people adapt to the climate and to life's complexities. I had known Toni in Vancouver when she was a "welfare Mom" with seven daughters, living in public housing. She had been a lead organizer for the Vancouver Opportunities Program, and had helped in my first campaign. Now she was Deputy Minister Responsible for Status of Women in the Territories, and had been a delegate to the Nairobi UN Status of Women conference. It was wonderful to see my old friend doing so well in her new circumstances. To top off my stay, Toni and the NDP women arranged a dogsled ride for me on Great Slave Lake—a great memory!

From Ottawa to Home

Stanley Knowles, our long-time House Leader who was respected by all parties, was incapacitated by a stroke and finally retired—or so we thought. When Trudeau made him an Honorary Clerk, Stanley took it seriously. He proceeded to dominate TV coverage each day as he sat at the Clerk's Table. He also refused to give up his offices and secretary. No one had the courage to restrict him, not even the Sergeant-at-Arms.

In 1984 Stanley asked me to arrange for him to visit Grace MacInnis, who was in a nursing home in Sechelt. I drove him there and we were warmly welcomed. When Stanley talked repeatedly about his brain, which had been injured by his stroke, Grace finally said, in her bossy way, "Stanley, I don't want to hear any more about your brain." Stanley was so shocked that his brain cleared and he made a wonderful speech to the patients. I loved them both.

In the House that same spring, I focused on education costs, peace, Vancouver Port proposals, family housing, preventive health care, and funding for multicultural programs. Summer's heavy schedule of pre-election legislation kept us very busy.

. . .

It was also a busy time on the home front. In Vancouver I organized a tour of women's centres with MLA Rosemary Brown. I had also met with women in Ottawa. The need for affordable, accessible, universal childcare was becoming a major issue in both cities, and I often raised it in speeches and reports.

Safety was also becoming more of an issue in parts of Vancouver. Violence involving knives was escalating in the Downtown Eastside. Leaders of DERA (the Downtown Eastside Residents Association), who were great organizers, held a forum with MLAs Mike Harcourt and Emory Barnes, Aldermen Harry Rankin and Bill Yee, and myself, to consider action. In Ottawa I called for changes to the Criminal Code to prohibit knives as a dangerous weapon.

DERA was also very concerned about the impacts of Expo '86. Tenants had been evicted from five housing projects when buildings were upgraded. Because of the community impacts, I opposed and boycotted Expo.

By 1986 the provincial political scene was changing again. Bob Skelly was elected as leader of the NDP, Glen Clark replaced Alex Macdonald as MLA for Vancouver East after a serious challenge by Margaret Birrell, whom I had supported. In Vancouver Centre Mike Harcourt replaced Gary Lauk. In 1987 the federal riding of Vancouver Kingsway was eliminated. Ian Waddell moved to Coquitlam and later went into provincial politics.

We deplored the harsh Social Credit and Conservative budgets that were cutting services and causing lost jobs. Postal services and Canada Employment services were also cut. I was particularly upset by the cuts in funding for the Native Education Centre in Vancouver, and for Women's Programs funding, which financed many supports and services for women, including women's centres.

Health Issues

Over the short time that I was Health Critic I focused mostly on preventive and women's health issues. I was building on the base set earlier by NDP Health Critic Bill Blakie from Manitoba, who had strongly supported the Canada Health Act, contributing many amendments to strengthen universal health care in Canada. That was during the time when the Minister of Health was Monique Bégin, a respected and progressive Liberal (whom I always thought should be a member of the NDP).

I continued to advocate for free access to abortion through hospitals and clinics, and I began to learn more about reproductive technologies that were becoming controversial. I also opposed government legislation that supported pharmaceutical companies and restricted less costly generic drugs.

As a strong supporter of community health clinics, I organized an extensive tour of clinics in my riding. One was a non-profit clinic that hired its own doctor. REACH (Research, Education and Action for Community Health) Clinic is a multilingual service in East Vancouver with adolescent services and counselling as well as dental and health services. Another that drew me was the Native Health Centre, established downtown to reach out to aboriginal street people. As Health Critic I advocated for an extension of Medicare to cover such non-profit clinics and to promote prevention, greater use of nurse practitioners, paraprofessionals, and alternate therapies. I felt that this would ease the load on doctors and cut costs. A team approach involving community people was needed.

I promoted the training and use of nurse practitioners to take over many of the chores of doctors in general practice in community clinics. This works in Canada's North—why not in the South? I realized that many of my interests in alternative delivery of medical services began in China in 1973 where "barefoot doctors" (who were dedicated community helpers) carried the front-line responsibility for keeping people healthy.

Child Care

The NDP made childcare a priority in our 1984 election platform. We felt that this should be a major national social program like Medicare, with national objectives. As many more mothers joined the workforce, Canadian women were expressing growing concern over the lack of adequate, affordable childcare in communities right across the country. NAC (The National Action Committee on the Status of Women) organized a nationally televised debate on women's issues in this election campaign and obtained a commitment from all three party leaders that action would be taken to improve childcare. Finally childcare had arrived on the political agenda.

After the 1984 election I was assigned the Child Care portfolio. Along with Hilary McMurray and NDP and CLC researchers, we developed a National Program for Child Care. We based it on seven principles— that services be comprehensive, quality, affordable, accessible, flexible, non-profit, and accountable. We pushed for $320 million in the 1987 federal budget so that we could begin to deal with the childcare crisis that was generating a lot of community interest. In response, I spoke to many groups and unions, and made a major presentation to National Association of Women and the Law.

In 1986 the Conservative government established a Parliamentary Special Committee on Child Care to study childcare needs and recommend action to the federal government. I was the NDP representative on this committee, which was chaired by Conservative MP Shirley Martin. Lucie Pepin was the Liberal representative, and two male Conservatives (Ross Belsher and Rob Nicholson) were added. UBC Social Work professor Dr. Glen Drover was the chief researcher for this committee.

Over many months we held public hearings in all regions of Canada and met many parents, grandparents, daycare providers, and child advocates who wanted comprehensive childcare to meet the needs of families in the '80s. A vocal minority shared the opinions of REAL Women, who felt women should stay at home and look after their children full time. Health and Welfare Minister Jake Epp and the Conservative majority on the committee encouraged this view, ignoring the economic needs of mothers to work. It was clear that the Tories had been opposed to a public childcare program from the beginning.

In the course of the committee's work we travelled to many rural and urban communities and heard many stories of the childcare crisis. Most parents were using unlicensed arrangements, unreliable care by a relative, or no supervision at all for school-age kids. Trained childcare workers, in a most important job, were earning only minimum wage. The few licensed group daycare centres that existed had long waiting lists or fees so high that most parents could not afford them. Licensed care for children under three was practically non-existent. I found the stories heartbreaking. It was very frustrating that governments were not supporting childcare as an essential service. Why was this, I wondered? Was it because childcare was seen largely as a "women's issue" and men rarely were active as advocates for daycare?

Partisanship was put aside as I became friends with other committee members. I especially enjoyed Liberal Sheila Finestone (sub for Lucie Pepin), who had been in Nairobi with me. On one occasion, the two of us had a long night at Vancouver airport waiting to fly to Whitehorse. Since the lounge was locked, they put us in the children's nursery, where I slept curled up in a kid's cot. I was amused the next day in Whitehorse when Sheila, not recognizing his red Liberal tie, tore strips off a presenter for being so reactionary. She was amazed when I congratulated her for trying to make a Liberal more progressive.

Working with the committee had its ups and downs. At one point I upset Glen Drover, who was my friend as well as the researcher for the committee. Frustrated by delays, I threatened to boycott the committee unless they made funding of licensed childcare services a priority. The Conservatives refused to consider government-subsidized childcare, despite the evidence of a Southam poll that found 60 percent of men and 66 percent of women supported government funding of daycare services. I also pressed for extensions to maternity and parental leave for those on Unemployment Insurance. The committee's only solution to the childcare crisis was tax write-offs for daycare fees. I argued that this would not create more daycare spaces, and would certainly not help lower-income parents.

It was apparent that philosophical differences with the Conservatives would prevent the committee from ever reaching consensus. In the end, the NDP refused to support the Special Committee Report, and my office prepared an NDP Minority Report based on our earlier proposals for a National Child Care Program.

When the Conservative government eventually drafted a Child Care Act in the early 1990s, it was only the skeleton of what was needed. It had no national objectives, would not increase childcare spaces, would encourage commercial childcare, and would withdraw Canada Assistance Plan coverage for the poor. Forty expert witnesses joined us in condemning this act. The government delayed a parliamentary vote on this bill and it eventually died on the Order Papers.

I was deeply disappointed that after so many months of consultation and work, no action was taken. Worst of all, I knew that the next generation of Canadian children would be denied adequate, affordable childcare, and mothers, many of them single parents on welfare, would be denied opportunities to work.

Buried in Snow

Claude was right—Ottawa was "blizzardly cold in winter and hot as hell in summer." Flying back from Vancouver in February and March, MPs were often detoured by storms to Toronto or Montreal and forced to finish the late-night trip by train or bus. Fearing the huge snowbanks and icy streets, I left my car in my apartment parking area over winter and used taxis.

One spring when it started to thaw, my friend who drove the little green bus on Parliament Hill came to my office. "Mrs. Mitchell," he said, "Is that your red car in the parking lot?" Sure enough, in my typical absent-minded fashion, I had left my car there all winter. It was only when the snowbanks began to thaw that my little red Honda was revealed. I got in, she started up immediately, and we drove off together to enjoy the spring.

By-election Success

In the fall of 1987, the NDP was successful in three by-elections. Marion Dewar was elected in Hamilton Mountain, Jack Harris in Newfoundland, and Audrey McLaughlin in Yukon. With Lynn McDonald, who had been elected earlier in Toronto, we now had a caucus of five women. When it came time for critic changes I suggested that Marion, who had been a very progressive mayor of Ottawa, assume Status of Women. It was time for a change. I retained the Health and Welfare portfolio and remained heavily involved in the Child Care Committee.

Parliament sat all during the hot, busy summer of 1988. I asked for federal funding for school food programs and opposed cuts to native and multicultural groups. I advocated funding for AIDS programs and parental leave for fathers. I proposed measures to end poverty and promote employment. However, I could have saved my breath since the Tories refused to respond to any progressive measures.

In Vancouver East I organized a "Celebration 88" event, inviting MLAs Bob Williams and Glen Clark to join me in recognizing many volunteers who had given years of service in their community. Outstanding volunteers were nominated by community groups and included a broad ethnic mix. We praised volunteers and presented them with medals at a large gathering at a Neighbourhood House. It was a very moving event. I realized how rarely citizens are thanked for their efforts.

Korean Pilgrimage

In 1988 Veterans Affairs Minister George Hees organized a pilgrimage of Canadian veterans to Japan and Korea. I was invited. It was hard to realize it had been thirty-five years since the truce. When we arrived at the Korean Demilitarized Zone, it could have been 1953. US and South Korean soldiers faced North Koreans across the border in silent hostility, ready for battle. I was sick at heart that peace was so unattainable. I will always remember the haunting lament of bagpipes from the hillside as we visited former battle sites where Canadian soldiers had died. I renewed my commitment to oppose war and work for peace.

CHAPTER 18

Canada's First Woman Leader

Although women's rights were high on the NDP agenda, caucus decisions were dominated by men. Several power-hungry men dominated executive positions, assigning duties as well as privileges, such as trips.

When female representation increased to five, Audrey McLaughlin, Lynn McDonald, Marion Dewar, Pauline Jewett, and I decided it was time to have a greater impact. We were actively recruiting women to run in the next election. When we began to caucus around the round table in the Opposition Lounge, the guys began to wonder what we were plotting. When we moved into the "Ladies Lounge," things got serious. (This lounge was originally provided for the sole use of wives of MPs—much to Claude's disgust.)

We realized that in order to have a greater say in decisions we would have to undertake leadership roles. The first step was to pass a motion recognizing "parity," which was party policy requiring gender parity in key positions. This passed in caucus. To implement this with a minority of women, we decided to each run for a senior position on the executive. Audrey was elected chair and I was elected whip. The other three women also took on senior roles. And so the feminist revolution took place.

It was a little while before our colleagues recognized that a coup had taken place. However, they soon began to feel the impact as we feminized the agenda and the style of operation with more group consensus in caucus and less belligerence in the House. In 1988 the NDP had been at its peak under Ed Broadbent's leadership. We won 20.5 percent of the national vote and 43 seats in the 1988 federal election. But there still were only five women NDP Members of Parliament. In 1989 after Ed Broadbent retired, our women's strategy was expanded. We decided to work within the party for nomination of a woman leader.

• • •

My life changed during the 34th Parliament. There was no joy in Ottawa after Mulroney's Conservatives were re-elected. They proceeded to implement NAFTA, which forced fish plants to close down, putting many Vancouver East people out of work, cancelled the Polar 8 icebreaker contract, which could have saved shipbuilding in Vancouver, imposed the GST, a regressive Goods and Services Tax, and, ignoring our months of hard work on the Special Committee on Child Care, ensured another generation of children would suffer, abandoned by the government. It was heartbreaking.

I still loved Vancouver East and politics, but I felt that a new generation had been elected and it was time to share responsibilities. I also wanted to have more time with Claude, who was seriously ill. I decided to step down as caucus whip to make way for newcomers. I took on a less demanding critic area, but one of great interest to me—Multiculturalism.

Leadership Changes

I was shocked when Ed Broadbent announced in 1988 that he was retiring as NDP Leader. He had been at his peak of popularity before the election and was optimistic that we could make inroads in Quebec. Unfortunately, this influenced him to modify his position on free trade. Our caucus had strongly opposed free trade, but it had many supporters in La Belle Province. When Ed and his staff decided unilaterally to appeal to Quebeckers by modifying his stance, many labour and party supporters were furious. Bob White, President of the CLC, was openly critical of Ed's campaign. When it was over, Ed's senior staff resigned, and soon Ed made his own announcement.

This was very disappointing to our caucus MPs, and I am sure it must have been very difficult for Ed. He had brought our party to a peak of popularity and was respected as a parliamentarian throughout Canada.

Ed went on to accept an appointment as head of the newly established Human Rights Commission. Many years later, in 2004, he had a brief return to public office as the very popular MP for Ottawa Centre.

After Ed stepped down, the battle to nominate a new NDP leader began. Our Women's Caucus still totalled only five, since Lynn McDonald and Marion Dewar had been defeated and Pauline Jewett had retired. They were replaced by Dawn Black, Lynn Hunter and Joy Langan from British Columbia. I was now called the Dean of Women, or "Deanery." (However, Dawn refused my counselling when I told her that her mini-skirt was too short.)

A Woman Leader

Our Women's Caucus was determined to see a woman running for the job. We were stronger, we had a more prominent leadership role in our caucus executive, and we set out to find the right woman. Eventually we persuaded Audrey McLaughlin to run. She was a Yukon MP and caucus chair. She had not had long parliamentary experience, but she was a committed socialist and feminist, was bright, well-organized, and attractive, and, like us, wanted to see changes in our party. She was my good friend and I decided to work hard for her.

Soon after, Lorne Nystrom and Simon de Jong of Saskatchewan and Ian Waddell of BC declared, followed by Stephen Langdon and Howard McCurdy from Ontario. Finally Dave Barrett, considered the man to beat, threw his hat in the ring. This presented a dilemma for me, since Dave had been our BC leader and had represented Vancouver East provincially. However I was committed to supporting Audrey.

As the leadership campaign progressed, tensions increased. Most of the BC men in caucus supported Dave and most unions in BC endorsed him (with the exception of the Steelworkers, who were backing Audrey). The pressures were on. CLC staffer Art Kube blocked our entry to the convention and threatened to deny financial support for Audrey supporters. Despite this intimidation we maintained our solidarity, led by the marvellous Yukon women who carried "AM for PM" signs. The vote was very close, but Audrey, with Stanley Knowles at her side, was elected our new leader. Dave refused to accept my handshake and never forgave me.

After the euphoria, the reality of rebuilding caucus relationships faced us. Audrey made sure those who had opposed her were not penalized for doing so. Dave's supporters had key positions on the caucus executive, but they continued to undermine Audrey or her staff. I missed the old camaraderie that I had enjoyed with male colleagues.

However, the whole women's agenda had progressed, and our Women's Caucus was pleased that our party was now really focused on equality. Our style had changed, too. Audrey was insistent that we try to be less confrontational in Parliament, which amused our male colleagues, who liked the old raucousness. Nonetheless, we didn't pound the desk as much and we were more civilized.

Audrey made many positive changes, raised important issues, and showed considerable patience and courage. She gained considerably more strength in caucus when she took a strong stand opposing the government involvement of the armed forces during the Oka Crisis in Quebec in 1990. But as usual, the media paid little attention to a woman politician. It was tough being the first woman in Canadian history to lead a federal party.

Wars at Home and Abroad

In 1989 the Montreal massacre of female students at L'école Polytechnique was the beginning of a cycle of violence that was followed by two wars. The Oka civil war in Quebec and the first Gulf War made our caucus realize our common support of peace and our belief in Canada's commitment to the United Nations. We united behind Audrey McLaughlin's leadership.

The Montreal Massacre

On December 6, 1989, Marc Lepine gunned down 14 women at the L'école Polytechnique at the University of Montreal. To many women, this massacre of female engineering students was symptomatic of the violence in society, especially the violence against women who entered the world of men. I could not comprehend a level of hatred against women that could result in such carnage. An unforgettable tragedy!

I joined Audrey, Dawn Black and Joy Langan in attending the very moving memorial service in Montreal for the victims of the massacre. Dawn had presented a motion, which was passed in Parliament, making

December 6 a national Day of Remembrance. In Vancouver, my office became the headquarters for a fundraising campaign in support of a memorial to be established in the park in front of the Pacific Central train station at Terminal and Main. Later I joined Vancouver women and the mothers of the victims to commemorate a circle of 14 plaques dedicated to the memory of the young women who had been slaughtered.

The First Gulf War

In 1989 Iraq invaded Kuwait. The general UN consensus was that tough sanctions would eventually force Iraq to withdraw. While agreeing to sanctions, the US began a tremendous build-up of military strength in the Gulf. In early 1990 America unilaterally started military action.

In the House of Commons, we strongly opposed a declaration of war by Canada, and advocated stronger sanctions and diplomacy. Audrey argued that war would take a huge human toll, killing Allied and Iraqi forces and civilians. It would bring environmental damage, and have a destabilizing effect on the region. "You can rarely promote peace by making war," she said. I remembered the futility and tragedy of the Korean War. When the votes in the House were counted, the NDP stood alone in opposing the government resolution to go to war.

As the devastation in Kuwait mounted, we urged the government to support new attempts at negotiating an end to the war. An estimated 170,000 children would die because of postwar conditions. The Middle East suffered a major environmental disaster as oil well fires spread horrific pollution. The US military might have "won," but Saddam Hussein's regime remained in power.

Oka

While conflagrations in the Middle East continued, a civil war broke out in Canada, which was a disgrace to our proud tradition as a peaceful nation. I felt sick and disgusted that we could not resolve differences peacefully.

In the summer of 1990, Prime Minister Mulroney ordered the Canadian Army to intervene in the Oka standoff in Quebec. It began when Kanesatake Mohawk warriors barricaded sacred land, which was about to be developed for a golf course. Sureté du Québéc officers confronted the warriors, using tear gas. When this led to a gun battle, a corporal was killed. Then Kahnawake Mohawks joined the Oka blockade and blocked a major bridge into Montreal.

When the provincial and federal ministers refused to intervene and the Sureté prevented food delivery or movement of people, Audrey decided to act. With two of her staff she took a van-load of food to the Oka community. For two days they were refused entry by police. Eventually they left the food nearby for pick-up, and Audrey entered the reserve to consult with Mohawks.

We strongly objected when Mulroney arbitrarily sent in the Canadian Army and dispersed the blockades. In her book *A Woman's Place: My Life and Politics*, Audrey said, "Our government was deploying troops against our own citizens. How could my country have come to this?" Like other blockades in Canada, this protest arose out of the refusal of authorities to respect aboriginal land claims. It was an expression of feelings of powerlessness. The standoff would never have reached the point of violence if authorities had talked and negotiated instead of calling in armed police and soldiers. Although the blockade was ultimately dispersed, anti-government feelings had increased and land claims remained unsettled.

CHAPTER 19

The Canadian Constitution: Meech Lake and Charlottetown

Amendments to the Charter of Rights and patriation of the Canadian constitution from England in 1982 were dramatic achievements of Prime Minister Pierre Trudeau. He was a brilliant scholar, but his arrogance defeated him in the end. The exclusion of Quebec from the final consensus was a devastating blow to Canadian unity and to future co-operation between the "two founding nations." It remained a blot on the Trudeau Liberal record, one which many Quebeckers would never forget or forgive.

Although constitutional issues were of little interest to the average Canadian, they became a major challenge for both Liberal and Conservative governments and for those of us who were NDP Members of Parliament during the 1980–1993 period. I was drawn into the debate to fight for women's equality, and I learned a great deal in the process.

Ed Broadbent was deeply committed to constitutional reform, and he worked for improvements in co-operation with both Mulroney and Trudeau. He became very emotionally involved in promoting the Meech Lake Accord, which many western New Democrats opposed. I found myself caught in the middle—supporting the caucus position while trying to explain it to my constituents and to members active in the women's movement.

Although most Canadians eventually expressed their disagreement with the amended constitution in a referendum vote, the years of study and compromise are an important part of our Canadian history. I include highlights of this struggle to show how it affected one MP—me.

When Prime Minister Brian Mulroney came to power with strong support from Quebec, including some separatists, he was determined to open the constitutional quagmire because Quebec had been left out of the first round of negotiations. By 1987, the Meech Lake Accord was drafted, recognizing Quebec as a "Distinct Society." We strongly supported this goal for Quebec because it recognized the different languages, culture, and legal system of Quebec. From his retirement in Quebec, former Prime Minister Pierre Trudeau strongly objected. However, many westerners later opposed the concept of a distinct society as catering to Quebec, while Quebec separatists saw themselves as a distinct nation that should be a sovereign country separate from Canada.

Pauline Jewett, our Constitutional Critic, speaking in Parliament, welcomed Quebec's return to the constitutional family with these words: "We have always felt it was a grievous occasion in 1982 when Quebec was isolated from patriation. As a party we have known that Quebec is indeed a distinct society and the linguistic duality of Canada is a vital characteristic of our nation. The Accord reunites Canada in a spirit of co-operative federalism."

In my speech to the House on October 8, 1987, I criticized the undemocratic process used to develop the Meech Accord. "We should remember that in the decisions behind closed doors at Meech Lake there were no Natives, northerners, women or disabled persons present. Decisions were made by eleven men—all white. This resulted in serious flaws which can be corrected by our three amendments."

I also objected to spending powers that would allow provinces to opt out of programs such as a National Child Care program. "Women's organizations fear that sexual equality may be at risk under the new Accord. They request a national women's conference and a referral to the Supreme Court to deal with their concerns," I argued.

Following approval by Parliament, a committee chaired by Conservative Justice Minister Jean Charest (who later became the Liberal premier of Quebec) travelled across Canada to get wider input from Canadians. Quebec Premier Robert Bourassa and Prime Minister Mulroney promptly opposed the Charest Committee's recommendations.

The PM, who preferred "cutting deals," went back to his secret negotiations and manipulations, and a complex resolution finally was ready for approval by provincial legislatures. In the end, the Meech Lake Accord was defeated by the single "No" vote, sustained with a feather, cast by Elijah Harper, the aboriginal NDP MLA from Manitoba. He raised a symbolic feather to express the strong opposition of his people.

Mulroney was devastated by the defeat of "Meech" and the subsequent angry defection of his friend Lucien Bouchard to the Bloc Québécois. He went into seclusion. Ed Broadbent, who had been a very strong advocate of the Meech Lake Accord, was also very disappointed. I was depressed by the divisions between the people in my riding

The Charlottetown Round

Despite his earlier failed agenda, Mulroney was determined to change the constitution. In 1992, he made another attempt at compromise in what became known as the Charlottetown Round. This time a national referendum was to be held so that Canadian people could vote on constitutional change. There was a little for everyone in his proposal, but not enough to satisfy anyone. The Distinct Society clause remained, the Triple E Senate was watered down to please Ontario, provinces were given more powers, a Social Charter proposed by the NDP was added, and Quebec was given a veto. As a caucus we were committed to "Yes." We felt aboriginal rights to self-government, an elected Senate, and a Social Charter were progressive steps for Canada. Unfortunately, many New Democrats did not agree.

In 1992 the NDP in Vancouver East led the push within the party for amendments to the Charter, seeking greater protection for minority rights from Clause 33, the "Notwithstanding Clause," which gave power to provinces to opt out of Charter rights. Tommy Tao and Allen Donavon prepared an excellent brief that expressed concern at the lack of protection for minorities. It was accepted by the party.

As soon as the referendum was announced, constituents began to complain. Again, women's groups were opposed, fearing their rights were not protected. The BC NDP Party was opposed. I had no heart for the "Yes" campaign, which required an alliance between Conservative and NDP MPs. Many of my supporters would vote "No." When the final votes were counted, the referendum was soundly defeated. I felt very depressed and hoped never again to be involved in constitutional reform.

Lighter Moments

Although my life as a politician had its disappointments, it also had its lighter moments. One of my greatest weaknesses as a politician was the difficulty I had remembering names. I asked my staff to help me. Gloria Levi advised me that I should memorize a new name by associating it with a familiar one. I tried this with a Mr. Gill whom I had met on the plane and invited to my office. Several times I prepared myself by repeating "Gill = fish, Gill = fish." When he arrived, I rushed forward, saying, "Come in, Mr. Fish. Welcome to Ottawa." When I realized my mistake, I had to excuse myself, and once out of sight, convulsed with laughter.

While I never became much better with names, over the years I learned various ways to compensate until I could remember a familiar face. I was told that Progressive Conservative leader John Diefenbaker used to cover up his lack of recognition by saying to people, "Hello, there. And how's the old complaint?" Naturally they were flattered that he remembered their lumbago and John became famous for remembering names.

Caucus members were often a source of fun, especially my seatmate, Jim Fulton, MP for Skeena. Once when he decided it was time to make an emphatic statement about the Tory mismanagement of BC fisheries, he enlisted my help. I was given a large BC salmon to hold while Jim completed his question to the PM. Receiving the expected unsatisfactory answer, Jim then grabbed the salmon from me, marched across the aisle, and deposited it on the PM's desk.

That caused an uproar, since it was against House rules to use props. Tories shouted their disgust that "a dead fish had been thrown at the PM." Afterward, Jim persuaded a page to sneak into the Tory lounge and rescue the dead fish so he could cook it for dinner. "No point in wasting a good BC salmon," he said.

I was amused at the contrasting reactions from people from the East and the West. Easterners were disgusted at Jim's behaviour while westerners loved it. The Nisga'a in Jim's Skeena riding embellished the fish story with many variations. One later version had me pulling the fish out of my dress.

IPU Conference in Cameroon

Inter-Parliamentary Union conferences provided a forum for Parliamentarians from around the world to share information, discuss issues, and have a good time. My final trip to Africa was to an IPU conference in bilingual Cameroon. As at most conferences, I socialized with labour delegates from other countries and sought out the few women MPs to promote women's participation.

This conference was delayed for several days by the President of Cameroon, who acted like an arrogant potentate. I wondered if his fabulously luxurious palace was paid for by Canadian aid. I was learning first-hand how the World Bank controlled Third World developments. Women who desperately needed funds for village survival programs found that World Bank finances usually went to useless mega-projects that benefited donor countries.

During the conference I made a special friend of Solange Gemayel, a Lebanese woman MP. She was the widow of the past president of Lebanon, who had been assassinated soon after he was elected. She replaced him as MP. We made a project of encouraging the all-male Japanese delegation to include women next time. It was when I was with Solange that I was shocked into realizing the irreparable divisions in the Middle East. When an Israeli woman MP came up to talk to me, my Lebanese friend said strongly, "Why don't you work for peace?" and violently turned her back on her. On my way home I visited Solange in Paris, where she lived in the most luxurious apartment I have ever seen.

CHAPTER 20

Personal Loss Shadows Multicultural Gains

Since my early travels in the Far East and South Pacific I have been interested in multiculturalism, and immigrants from all over the world have settled in Vancouver East. I once counted 17 different nationalities after canvassing two streets in my neighbourhood. Earlier immigrants from Italy were being replaced by Asian immigrants from Hong Kong, China, Vietnam, Taiwan and Korea. Indo-Canadians moved to South Vancouver, while Latin Americans from Central and South America found refuge in the downtown area. Spanish-speaking constituents offered help in Spanish out of my office.

I had friends in all ethnic communities and I attended many cultural events. I empathized with refugees who were refused entry to Canada. Lil Reid Smith and I helped win appeals for many. I found the diversity in Vancouver East to be stimulating and enriching. It was heartwarming to visit schools and see the inter-racial mix of children from different backgrounds. They were becoming Canadians, not hyphenated Chinese-Canadians or Italian-Canadians. Increasingly over the years, the majority of students were persons of colour. I rarely had complaints about racism, although ethnic youth gangs were a concern.

Liberal multicultural policy had welcomed immigrants and encouraged ethnic programs with special grants. Trudeau had introduced multiculturalism, perhaps to counterbalance bilingualism. Conservatives continued this vote-getting policy and they established a Multicultural

Committee (that rarely met). I pressed for an active Parliamentary Committee that would redefine multiculturalism and monitor employment equity.

I felt strongly that the NDP needed to work aggressively to become more inclusive. From the time that the CCF pressed for and won the right for Asian and aboriginal Canadians to vote, we had been strong advocates for human rights. But it was hard to attract immigrants, many of whom had fled communist regimes, to join a socialist party that was not likely to be the party in power federally.

Despite our limited ability to attract immigrants to the party, I felt it was time to update our NDP multicultural policy with emphasis on human rights and anti-racism programs. Employment equity needed to be enforced to bring about greater equality in federal jobs and systemic change in our federal institutions. My goals also included a plan to encourage greater diversity in the NDP, to remind Canadians of historic injustices that needed redress, and to celebrate cultural events within the wider community. I tried to promote the idea that all Canadians are "multicultural." This was becoming a characteristic of Canadian citizenship.

One of the reforms that Audrey McLaughlin implemented in the NDP was to entrench multiculturalism as a party policy. I worked on this with Howard McCurdy, a black MP from Windsor who had wide experience fighting for minority rights. Together we organized our party's own federal Multicultural Committee. We were looking for ways to reach out to and involve minorities in the NDP, and to encourage systemic change in provincial and constituency associations, which were predominantly white. A new Affirmative Action policy was passed, requiring a certain percentage of Federal Council officers to represent minorities, including aboriginal people.

We held a well-attended multicultural workshop at the federal NDP convention that had excellent participation from minority groups. Participants became an action cadre, carrying out strategies in local ridings, including the recruitment of minority candidates to run for nominations. I frequently raised these issues in the BC Party. At one point I organized a meeting of Chinese, Black and South Asian members to discuss racism with the provincial Minister of Multiculturalism. They cited many examples of incidents of racism they had experienced. It was an emotional meeting, and at one point the Minister broke down in tears.

Wendy Jang had come to Ottawa from Vancouver to work full-time as my Multicultural Assistant. We worked closely with the Canadian Ethno-cultural Council, a federation of major Canadian ethno-cultural organizations. The council was a strong advocacy group to government, and they fed us issues of concern from their affiliates for us to raise in the House. In turn, I spoke at their meetings and press conferences.

Wendy prepared a regular NDP newsletter on multiculturalism that we sent to an increasingly wide circulation. She also did a lot of work with multicultural groups in Vancouver during summer breaks. Glen Sanford also worked for me in this period, both in Ottawa and as an organizer in the riding. His journalistic and organizing skills continued to be very valuable to me and to the NDP.

Redress

As Canadians, we pride ourselves on being a tolerant nation, but the more I learned about Canada's racist history, the more determined I was to puncture the complacency of Canadians. I believe we must all become more aware of our history, appreciate the contribution various cultures have made to Canada, and recognize the need for redress of past injustices.

However, in Parliament it was difficult to get questions in my critic area or to attract publicity. I continued to press for redress for people who paid the racist Chinese Head Tax, and often raised this in Chinese New Year statements. The Conservatives ignored the Chinese, but were more responsive than the Liberals regarding redress for Japanese Canadians. Their compromise settlement included funds for a Race Relations Institute to be established in Toronto.

I celebrated with my Vancouver friends of Japanese origin. I was particularly touched by the meaning this government apology had in relieving the unwarranted feelings of guilt experienced by many elders who had suffered discrimination and displacement during World War II. I enjoyed making a friend of writer Joy Kogawa, who had been a child victim of Canada's racist policy.

Canada's history has been marred by other injustices against ethnic groups, and I raised these in speeches and in Parliament. Sikhs in Vancouver had made me aware of Canada's refusal to accept refugees from India who arrived in the Port of Vancouver early in this century on the ship the *Komagata Maru*. While there was already a thriving South Asian community in Vancouver, after 1907, restrictions made it impossible for any new immigrants to arrive from India. Those aboard the *Komagata Maru* were confined to the ship for two months while the local Sikh community raised money for food, and to fight the legal battle to have those on shipboard allowed into the country. They lost.

On our East Coast, prior to World War II, a shipload of Jewish refugees was refused entry to Canada by Prime Minister McKenzie King. They were forced to return to the Nazi Holocaust. Ukrainian Canadians were interned in World War I and German and Italian Canadians were incarcerated without trial during World War II. Schoolchildren need to be made aware of these injustices.

Racism and Hatred

As well as raising human rights issues in the House and in speeches on International Day to Eliminate Racism, I pushed for enforcement of the Employment Equity Act so that our civil service would become more representative of the Canadian mosaic. People of colour and aboriginals were grossly under-represented. I also raised cases of discrimination against highly qualified immigrants who were refused promotions in the public service, and I deplored the strict restrictions that prevented professionals from working in their field in Canada.

It was difficult to deal with hate propaganda in Canada, since our Charter protects freedom of speech. The America-linked Neo-Nazi movement was growing in Canada, spreading hatred, particularly against Jews. When I raised a strong objection in the House to the planned appearance of a British Holocaust denier in Ottawa, I was immediately flooded with e-mail messages from across the US and Canada, claiming that I was denying the democratic right to free speech. I, too, had become the victim of hatred. I called for changes to the Criminal Code to deal with hate propaganda.

I had been formulating a new NDP multicultural position, which

I wanted to enunciate in a speech to the National Jewish Congress in Toronto. I hated to leave Claude, who was seriously ill with cancer, but I felt this was an important finale to my work. The speech was well received.

Claude

Claude had mellowed over the years—was less noisy and aggressive. He maintained his Aussie independence and his own circle of friends, and in many ways, because of my absence, we lived separate lives. He was very fond of our friend Mary Lee and her two daughters, Dora and Martina, and Mary kept an eye on him for me as well as doing our cleaning.

When the dark, rainy weather hit Vancouver, Claude missed the sun and heat of his native Australia. Most Christmases we headed for Mexico to enjoy the sun and the friendly Mexican people, and so that Claude could practise his Spanish.

Claude loved Mexico and he visited it often, sometimes on his own and sometimes with me. I was hurt the first time he went without me, but later realized this was probably a time in his life when he needed to reassert his independence. He liked to roam around on his own, talking with local people who responded to his outgoing humour. I travelled with him many other times and we visited a number of different regions.

The beach tourist centre of Mexico did not appeal to us, but on one trip to Mazatlan we enjoyed a visit from my niece Jane. This was quite an adventure for her, as she almost missed connecting with us. Then she shared the sole bed and homemade meals in our tiny hotel room, and was introduced to bullfighting—with Claude's commentary. Another trip started in Manzanillo, where we stayed in a cheap room and hung out in the plaza, talking to children and their parents. A young man befriended us, took us home to his parents' house, and insisted we stay for New Year's Eve dinner. We also enjoyed the beautiful parks, art collections and historic buildings of Guadalajara City, "the Paris of Mexico."

I especially remember Mexico City—the crowds, the beggars at every corner, and the magnificent central square encircled with markets, the cathedral, and government buildings. We always visited the Diego Rivera murals in City Hall, which document Mexican revolutionary history so dramatically.

It was in the mid '80s when the two of us were in Oaxaca to explore ancient ruins that Claude first suffered from stomach pains, which curtailed his activities. I was unaware for some months that this was the first sign of colon cancer. A first operation seemed successful. Soon afterward, Claude purchased the Mayne Island house, which he said would make it easier for my sister Betty and me to get together since she lived on nearby Saturna Island. He also needed a more comfortable indoor bathroom, which we didn't have on Salt Spring. The three-bedroom Mayne Island house was great for family and group gatherings, and Claude worked to finish off recreation rooms in the basement. He and our next-door neighbour, Ted McGiveron, became great pals, shouting insults at each other in true Aussie fashion. Ted was a true Canadian, but he soon learned to match Claude's penchant for kidding insults.

Looking back, I think we were both in denial and unfortunately did not discuss his illness openly. When his health worsened, I realized it was time to scale back my own activities. I arranged to be home for three days each weekend, and under the new parliamentary schedule we now had one week a month in the riding.

Claude refused to have anyone live in or come in to help him, and he often left untouched the frozen meals I prepared for him. He insisted that I continue my work, and I really wanted to—all the while feeling guilty. He kept in touch with friends and often went over to work on projects on Mayne Island. We talked each day, but he no longer met me at the airport when I came home on weekends.

Claude still was very supportive and proud of my work as an MP. He continued to help in many practical ways to ease pressures. When I was in Ottawa he loved to represent me at community events—especially at Chinese dinners. People loved him for his humour. But knowing Claude, I was a bit nervous when he decided to make a speech.

As Claude's illness progressed, so did his reticence to discuss it. My response was denial, and I continued to be very busy. Fortunately, my schedule now allowed me more time at home. A second operation removed more of the colon. Once when I arrived home, Claude took me on his knee and tried to explain his feelings for me. All he could say was, "You were the only woman I ever wanted to marry." I told him I loved him, but we were unable to talk about his dying.

Betty joined us on Claude's final trip to Mexico. We were in Vera Cruz, where we stayed in a suite of rooms overlooking the very busy plaza. Claude was in considerable pain and we were unable to obtain a prescription for Tylenol 3 for him. We brought him meals from the square and he listened to music and watched activities from the balcony.

On leaving Vera Cruz, Claude insisted on walking through the airport security check, where we were deprived of our "honeymoon" camping knife. After we had cleared customs he collapsed on the stairs. The airport clinic staff provided wonderful treatment for his low blood sugar, and after several hours we were able to fly to Mexico City. Despite being very weak, Claude insisted on visiting the city's plaza to see the people selling and performing, to have a last look at his favourite Rivera murals, and to see the cathedral that was sinking from the recent earthquake. We took a last slow walk around the square. . . .

When I returned briefly to Ottawa, Claude, on morphine now, decided to take a last lonely trip to Mayne Island. After struggling up the steep hill, he sat in the cold house and talked on the phone to my sister Betty for an hour. Our neighbour Ted rescued him and drove him to the ferry. Our caucus whip arranged compassionate leave, and I was very relieved to be going home to Claude.

When Claude felt up to it, we visited old friends and places he loved. He hated to have me wait on him, and I worried that he was not eating. Community nurses dropped in periodically. In late September, I had to go overnight to Toronto to present our new NDP position on multiculturalism, something I had been working on for a while. When I anxiously phoned home, there was no answer. I called my friend Crissy George, who immediately went to the rescue. Claude was worse. Crissy contacted the doctor, who was able to get him into palliative care, and I flew home the next day.

I was filled with guilt. I spent most of my time at the hospital with Claude or hunting for the banana drink to which he had become addicted. He came home for a visit the next two weekends, and we had quality time together, despite his morphine state. A high point was visiting the old PNE carousel, which was being refurbished in the classical style he loved. I asked the two young Lee girls, who were with us, to choose a horse, and I made a contribution so that Claude could name it. He called it "Phar Lap," after the famous Australian race horse.

Our Australian friend Clare, her husband Lloyd Sturgeon, and Russian friend Nina Bell visited Claude on his birthday. We reminisced about old times and shared tears. Claude and I laughed together when neither of us could organize his various bags and tubes.

The next day Claude returned to the hospital and the morphine took over. On his last night, Patsy George stayed overnight at the hospital with me, and my nephew, David Speers, came early the next morning. Betty was in Nanaimo, assisting in the delivery of her son Ken's first daughter, Mariah. Overnight I held Claude's hand and told him I loved him. He squeezed my hand. And then he was gone.

Claude had not wanted a funeral. He always said, "Throw my bones in an old TV and toss it in the sea." For the rest of us, we had a memorial not soon forgotten. Shane Simpson helped to arrange it, and friends from all walks of life spoke lovingly of how Claude had helped them. A tough, burly motorcyclist from Claude's motorcycle club said emotionally, "I loved that guy."

Some months later in the summer I had a Mayne Island gathering of friends and relatives from Australia and California to spread Claude's ashes. I was so stressed out from arranging complex travel and food for the crowd that when I got on the ferry, I realized I had forgotten the ashes. The wonderful ship's purser arranged to collect and deliver the ashes from David Speers, saving the day. Later we had a good laugh about it together, imagining what Claude was likely saying about Marg's stupidity.

When Claude died, some of the joy went out of life, and so did some of my fighting spirit. I did not realize how stressed and weary and lonely I was until a week later when I returned to Ottawa. I arranged for a massage. The tears flowed for an hour. Despite our differences, through good times and bad, we had formed a strong and loving bond. His death left a huge hole in my life. It would be a long time before I returned to Mexico.

In December I sold our East End house and bought a waterfront False Creek condo, which was easier to maintain. I had always longed to live by water, but Claude had refused to move. Now I was where I had wanted to be, but was at a loss about my future. My English friend, Joan Waterfall, invited me to Wales and for Scottish dancing over Christmas. It was a much-needed break.

Some weeks later, I went to a Canadian Labour Congress and caucus retreat in Quebec. My colleagues welcomed me back, and I had a long walk and sympathetic talk with my Nairobi CLC friend, Diane Wood. I asked my friend Gordie Larkin if I should run again. He replied, "If it's what you want, we'll support you." I went home to discuss this with riding friends.

Other Losses

While Claude had been suffering from colon cancer in Vancouver, my close friend Pauline Jewett, now a retired MP, had developed lung cancer. When in Ottawa, I spent a lot of time with her, being ordered about willingly as one of several caregiver friends. I drove with her in her new "Jag" to her cottage, which she had had for many years in a community of Carleton University friends.

Journalist Marjorie Nichols had also become a close friend of Pauline's during the Meech Lake constitutional process, and helped her to stop drinking and smoking. Then Marjorie also developed cancer and predeceased Pauline. Doris Anderson frequently drove from Toronto to the cottage to be with her old friend. MP Marion Dewar, a natural caregiver and former nurse, took over when I went home to Vancouver in the summer. In her last days, Pauline Jewett received the Order of Canada. Prime Minister Mulroney also appointed her to the Privy Council for her work on constitutional reform. When she died, Pauline was sadly missed in both Vancouver and Ottawa.

IPU Conference in Hungary

In 1991 I was fortunate to be a Canadian delegate to the Inter-Parliamentary Conference in Hungary, which proved to be an historic time. I was very moved to finally see the homeland of the many refugees I had known in 1957 while I was working in a Hungarian refugee camp in Vienna. The Cold War was over, and now Hungary was preparing for democratic parliamentary elections.

I was asked to chair a session on Rights of the Child, and I presented a major paper, which was well received. The head of UNICEF asked me to persuade Prime Minister Mulroney to support the UN Resolution on Children's Rights. I had to admit that as an Opposition Member, I had little influence.

One evening during the conference, the 1956 Hungarian Revolution was remembered in a silent, candlelit vigil. Hundreds of people walked across the beautiful bridge that joins Buda to Pest. I joined the crowds to watch the ceremony in which the Soviet Union's hammer-and-sickle flag was removed from the Parliament buildings and replaced with the Hungarian flag. I remembered Hungarian refugees I had known in Vienna.

While in Budapest I also had an interesting and entertaining evening at a dinner hosted by the new Canadian Ambassador to Hungary and his wife. They seemed to give me an especially warm welcome. I was seated beside the Ambassador along with Hungarian VIPs and a Canadian Senator. The conversation turned to elections, and the Ambassador asked me to explain to the Hungarians what we did to get elected. I gave a brilliant and detailed description of nominating procedures, door-knocking canvasses, organizing a campaign, and getting the vote out. "It's fun," I said.

The very dignified older professor, who was a senior Hungarian scientist, looked pale, and said he could never do this. He had been appointed to the Hungarian Parliament and was terrified that now he would have to go through this strange election process. Someone asked the Canadian Senator how he was elected. This met with dead silence. The Senator finally had to admit that he, too, was not elected but appointed. I couldn't resist adding, "That's why my party wants to abolish the Senate."

I was in a fun mood and tried to persuade the stuffy Canadian Tories to follow Hungarian etiquette and kiss my hand. All but one succumbed. Our delegates visited both sides of the Danube and marvelled at the ancient beauty of Budapest. Sentimental memories of earlier times in Vienna flooded back when I heard Hungarian gypsy music and ate Hungarian goulash.

CHAPTER 21

The End of an Era

I missed having Claude to confide in and discuss my future. My closest advisors, Shane and Lil, thought I should run again. Many supporters had signed a petition urging me to run. I wanted to, but felt my age was a factor (I was 67 in 1992). Was I considering running again because of my own personal needs, or because there was no obvious replacement?

The 1993 Federal Election

Feeling ambivalent, I agreed to run—later tried to withdraw—but finally succumbed. I needed a strong campaign manager, and Ed Vaasenar, who had managed my first campaign, agreed to take on the job again.

Although we had lots of workers, I sensed there was less enthusiasm in our campaign. In addition to opposition to our party's stand on the Meech Lake Accord, many of my supporters felt strongly about our position on Clayoquot Sound logging. Environmentalists wanted a moratorium on clear-cut logging in this beautiful coastal area. Our caucus had accepted the provincial NDP position that a reasonable compromise had been reached between areas designated for logging and for environmental protection. During the campaign, I remained neutral. Should I have opposed the positions of both the provincial and federal NDP? I did not know enough to take a strong independent position, as fellow NDP MP Svend Robinson had done. I felt I had copped out by avoiding the issue.

I thought our campaign was going fairly well, but I was tired and anxious to have it over. My campaign manager gave me only positive feedback. On voting night, I dressed up for the post-election party and went to the campaign office to await results. My friend Shane Simpson came to sit beside me, saying, "It looks bad, Marg."

When the results came in, I had lost to the Liberal candidate, Anna Terrana, and the NDP had lost all but two seats in BC. The Conservatives under Kim Campbell had won only two federal seats. Gains of the Reform Party and the new Bloc Party, which became the Official Opposition, had given Jean Chrétien's Liberals a majority. Shane and I briefly left the "party," which had become a wake, to congratulate Anna.

Why did we lose the 1993 election? Obviously I had not been at my best, and probably should not have run. However, the national trends affected almost every riding. We lost some support of environmentalists who were mad at the provincial NDP. The Chinese community ran a well-financed campaign against Reform, fearing their anti-immigration policies. They urged people to get out to vote, and to vote Liberal. Many Canadians were fed up with politicians and politics after the Mulroney years, and probably didn't vote at all.

I was stunned by the results on election night and went home alone, feeling lonely, defeated, and depressed. I felt I had let my supporters down. Two days later after a long sleep I awoke feeling that a tremendous pressure had been lifted from my shoulders. A sense of freedom flowed through me. I realized that after fourteen years of politics, I was free at last to relax, to enjoy my new home, to get to know my sister Betty's ten grandchildren, and to have a life.

Looking Back

I wondered what I had accomplished during my time in office. I was not motivated by prestige or power. I was not a great orator or a mistress of the thirty-second clip. As Harold Winch had implied, I often was too humble. My strengths were my enjoyment of and respect for people, a strong commitment to my constituents, my persistent advocacy for poor people, for women, and for multiculturalism, and my belief in practical socialism. Most of the time, I enjoyed politics and respected my colleagues. Hard work and a sense of humour helped. But I hated the negative media stereotyping that portrayed us all as selfish pigs at the trough.

Margaret visited childcare programs across Canada with the Child Care Committee.

Members of the Four Sisters Co-op celebrate their 5th Anniversary:
(L-R) Amber Daniel, Barb Daniel, Margaret Mitchell and Maxine Gadd.
This housing co-op was developed by single mothers.

Visiting the Yucatan ruins with Crissy George and Patsy George

Betty's many Saturna Island friends send love to her in hospital.
Betty died on June 10, 2003.

Margaret (on
compassionate leave)
with Claude, who died
November 14, 1991.

Family party at Marg's condo: Jane Shepherd, Jack and Lori Speers, Richard
and Cody Shepherd, Sue Speers with Travis, Betty Speers with Justin
Tracy, David, and Jenna Speers

Receiving the Order
of BC medal from
Lieutenant Governor
Garde Gardom, 2000.

On returning to Korea in 1988 with Veterans Affairs Minister George Hees
and Korean War veterans, I was presented with the Korean War Service medal.

Betty at Saturna Island
Lamb Barbeque.

Claude campaigns
on motorcycle, 1983.

Betty Speers, Margaret Mitchell and Tracy Speers.

Celine Speers (left) with school friends on Saturna Island.

MP Sisters on Canada Day, 2003 at Saturna Lamb Barbeque: Audrey
McLaughlin, Dawn Black, Lynn Hunter, and Margaret Mitchell.

Betty Speers' cabin on Saturna Island, built with recycled wood.
Margaret's new extension is on the left.

DERA campaigns for Margaret (mid-1980s).

I was always surprised when, over the years, people came up to thank me for what I had done. I continued to receive a very warm reception at gatherings in Vancouver—balm to the soul of a retired politician. I was pleased when one constituent said, "Margaret, you raised the benchmark for integrity and hard work." Young women often came up to thank me for being a role model for them.

My efforts had not gone unnoticed in official circles, either. In 1996 I received the Helena Gutteridge Award for Community Service. Later I received awards from my alma mater, McMaster University, and also from Simon Fraser University, where Claude had established scholarships in my name. In 2000, attended by family and friends, I received the Order of British Columbia at Government House in Victoria. The Order of British Columbia statement reads as follows:

As a leader in social policy and women's rights, Margaret Mitchell put violence against women on the national agenda and played a critical role in having women recognized in the Charter of Rights and Freedoms. She pioneered community development in many Vancouver neighbourhoods, helping to organize public housing tenants and creating opportunities for people on welfare. She is a strong advocate for minority rights and multiculturalism.

Her outstanding work as a community development worker has inspired many social workers in BC to follow her path. Her book Don't Rest in Peace—Organize! *has been a beacon for community mobilization and empowerment.*

As the Member of Parliament for Vancouver East from 1979 to 1993 she voted against a pension increase for MPs and diverted her share of the increase to a special account to help the poorest in Vancouver's Downtown Eastside. With her support, the Margaret Mitchell Fund for Women continues to grow and assist women's organizations in East Vancouver dedicated to helping women help themselves in bettering their community. Her life has been dedicated to helping people, starting with her service with the Red Cross in Asia and Europe, where she helped refugees from war in their time of dire need.

Since her retirement from public service, she continues to serve British Columbia in many volunteer capacities, including being the first Chair of the BC Advisory Council on Human Rights.

SECTION 4

Retirement

CHAPTER 22

Retirement: False Creek, Friends, and Community

Nineteen ninety-three was my year of recovery and rejuvenation. "Do you miss being in politics?" people would ask. My answer was a decisive "No!" I had been privileged to enjoy a rare life experience as an elected representative—a fulfilling, exciting, and occasionally painful fourteen years. I had learned and developed a great deal and felt that I had represented my constituents well. But now I was free to "get a life." I developed a philosophy for retirement that included relaxing and enjoying life with time for family, friends, and new experiences. My goal was self-fulfilment and a healthy lifestyle, after a life of social responsibility.

False Creek Community

My move to South False Creek proved to be a good one. False Creek is a former industrial site that was redeveloped in the '60s as a mixed-income community with social housing, co-ops, and housing for seniors interspersed with expensive apartments and waterfront town houses. The creative planners and landscapers produced a pedestrian-oriented model community. I feel very fortunate to live there.

I love my two-bedroom condo, which has a glorious view of sea and sky and sunsets. I am within walking distance of all amenities. When I finish my shopping at the Granville Island Public Market, I take the rainbow ferryboat home, checking out the massive new developments across the creek on the old Expo '86 site.

Friends

Despite the joy of my new home, I soon found that retirement and my move out of Vancouver East (where I left my heart) meant a loss of contact with former political friends. At first I was lonely. Travels with sister Betty and visits to the Gulf Islands were diversions. However I soon realized I had to make new friends and take up new activities—a reality many widows must face.

To help control high blood pressure and osteoporosis, I limit coffee to a cup a day, avoid alcohol (no problem since alcoholic poisoning in Korea), make low-cholesterol meals, walk, and enjoy afternoon naps (a genetic inclination). I joined an osteofit class at the False Creek Community Centre. I was flattered when former acquaintances began to say I was looking younger. Increased energy was replacing stress.

I dabbled at line dancing, Tai Chi, and painting, but eventually focused on music, with a new appreciation of opera and the symphony. When on Mayne Island I played the piano. As a techno moron I was intimidated by my new Mac computer and had to rely on younger experts to help me. Eventually I learned to type and use e-mail, and I contemplated writing my memoirs.

At the False Creek Community Centre I made a new friend, Irene Craig, who lives in my condo building. We walk and talk, share laughs, and go to movies. We play bridge—for me a long-forgotten game—with Muren Shackter and Nan Ravvin, who also live in our building, making up a friendly foursome. We are less successful at seducing men.

I also made a close friend of Gloria Levi, who lives nearby and attended osteofit classes with me at the community centre. Gloria is an amazing woman, who in her late sixties started a very successful Habitat Housing program, while continuing religious studies and organizing a large family. In 2005 we travelled together to Morocco, visiting Audrey McLaughlin, and then explored Southern Spain.

Patsy George, who had been my friend and ally through community development, Vancouver Resources Board, and NDP days now lives in a nearby downtown condo. She and her sister Crissy continue to be my close friends. Patsy is a dinner party hostess, a travel companion, an opera organizer and an NDP associate. A year after I received an Order of BC medal in 2001, Patsy received hers. Crissy spent two years as a volunteer social worker in Belize. Along with Deepthi Jayatilaka, who came to live with Patsy, they are my guardian angels when they aren't travelling around the world.

Bessie Lee and I go to the symphony together and reminisce about old Strathcona days. Long-time friends Nora Curry and Marjorie Martin both live in Victoria now, but join us (and Darlene Marzari too) for most of these activities, including trips to Mayne for Scrabble binges. Since Pam (my friend from Red Cross days) and Dick McLeod moved from Ottawa to Victoria, we get together there or on Mayne Island, telling Korean War stories that are almost fifty years old now but are still alive for the two veterans.

On Mayne Island, Ted and Pat McGiveron keep watch over my house, and Terry Flatt, my volunteer "guerrilla gardener," keeps the grounds under control. Don Sampson, a socialist originally from Vancouver East, lives nearby. He became a friend and later joined our opera group. Once he called me to see a pod of thirteen orcas feeding off his point.

Next to my sister Betty, perhaps my dearest friends and confidantes are my MP "sisters"—Audrey McLaughlin based in Whitehorse, Lynn Hunter in Victoria and Dawn Black in Burnaby. We had been through intense struggles in the last Parliament, and all (except Audrey) had lost in the 1993 election. Lynn and Dawn had no pension or income or employment for months. Audrey unjustifiably assumed the blame for the NDP defeat, worked to renew the party, and eventually resigned. Lynn kept us connected by e-mail.

We met twice a year when we could connect with Audrey between her trips—usually at a resort or for a pyjama party at my place. We bonded, shared gossip, laughed a lot and provided sympathy and support when needed. When Audrey worked for the National Democratic Institute in Bahrain and Iraq in 2003 and 2004, we worried and wondered if workshops she led on democracy were worth the risks. We shared our anger that President Bush Jr. initiated a war that was a disaster for all participants. There is nothing quite like sisterhood for sharing concerns and support.

Community Involvement: SPARC, Premier's Forum, BCHRC

After years of intense social and political commitment, I decided I would only get involved with community organizations if I really wanted to take on a new responsibility. Although several interested me, I decided to limit my involvement to two organizations at a time.

SPARC of BC

I became a board member of SPARC and was active for several years. The Social Planning and Research Council of BC is a provincial organization committed to social justice, research and community development. An annual Community Development Institute brought together participants from around the province to learn from and share their community experiences. As an activist, I eventually found it frustrating to sit on a policy board that was not involved in direct action.

The Premier's Forum on Working and Living

In 1994 I was asked by Premier Mike Harcourt to be a member of the Premier's Forum on Working and Living. He established a large task force with wide representation from business, labour, universities and the community, primarily to review social services. Human Resources Minister Joy McPhail chaired the forum, and senior Ministers participated. Unfortunately, the forum did not live up to expectations.

When we considered social policy, the conflicting philosophies of participants emerged. The representative from End Legislated Poverty and I were the only advocates for poor people. I was frustrated that NDP policies were ignored. The discussion was dominated by three professors, who seemed to follow a right-wing Fraser Institute type of philosophy. I strongly objected when one wanted Workfare (working for welfare) as a welfare policy.

It was apparent that no consensus was possible with such a disparate group. I was amazed when Joy arbitrarily appointed the three right-wing professors to prepare a final report. I was even more amazed (and disgusted) when the report was accepted, even though it was never discussed by the forum. I subsequently asked the Premier to have my name removed from the document, and I wrote to both Joy and Mike, explaining my reasons for disagreeing. Out of loyalty to the party, I did not go public.

Most social workers and New Democrats objected to the punitive BC Benefits program, which subsequently was introduced as welfare reform.

The only positive aspect of it was a child tax credit for mothers going off welfare. In the following years, dependence on food banks soared as welfare rates were cut. I was convinced the regressive approach of BC Benefits had a direct impact on the increasing numbers of single unemployed persons who were homeless on our streets without social assistance. Begging and crime increased. I was ashamed for the NDP.

The BC Human Rights Commission

In 1998 I was appointed by NDP Minister of Justice Ujjal Dosanjh to be the first Chair of the BC Human Rights Advisory Council (BCHRAC). Working in a semi-government capacity to bring community input into the Human Rights Commission was a new experience for me. Our diverse committee travelled around the province to consult citizens.

We prepared regular reports for the Minister with recommendations for legislation and made some practical changes. Then Minister Dosanjh became a short-term Premier and lost the next election in 2001. The BC Liberals disbanded the Advisory Council, leaving only a tribunal in its place.

The Margaret Mitchell Fund for Women

After my retirement I decided to establish a Fund for Women, using the monies I had saved and invested from the MP pay raises I had opposed. I added extra funds, and eventually donated my waterfront property on Salt Spring Island, which was sold by the VanCity Foundation (the offshoot of VanCity Credit Union which manages the fund). The proceeds from the real estate added $220,000 to the fund, which soon totalled $247,000. The interest is used for grants.

To oversee the fund, I established an advisory committee of Van East women who are active in the community, including our new MP Libby Davies. Patsy George co-chaired. They named the fund and advised staff on projects that should be given priority for funding: programs and initiatives that promote economic and social justice for women in Vancouver East by alleviating poverty, promoting equality, and helping women to gain confidence and power. A scholarship fund for women attending the Native Education Centre also was designated.

In the first seven years of its operation, the fund disbursed $75,700, mostly to groups in the Downtown Eastside. Financial assistance has gone to groups and individuals seeking business training, promoting health among sex-trade workers, counselling for women in abusive relationships, and bursaries to support retreats for women.

The VanCity Community Foundation

Claude and I had been contributing members of the Vancouver City Credit Union (now VanCity) since the '60s. We both had savings accounts and investments there and believed in the co-operative credit union philosophy. In 1999, after I had established the Margaret Mitchell Fund for Women, which the VanCity Foundation administers, I was asked to be on the foundation board. I was delighted, as I am interested in the many practical community economic development enterprises which they financed and assisted.

It was refreshing to hear members of a large and successful financial institution espouse a social philosophy with a strong commitment to community economic development. Many people began to contribute to named funds during this period, increasing the capital endowment of the foundation. I was reminded of the co-operative community we had visited in Mondragon, Spain, and wished these models could be expanded in BC.

Simon Fraser University

Both Claude and I had a special relationship with Simon Fraser. After he retired, Claude established three scholarships at SFU—one for Chemistry, honouring his friend Marshall Noble, one for Women's Studies, and one for women in Political Science. The latter two go to women from Vancouver East. After I retired I was invited to several SFU events and received a Community Service Award. I sponsored the refurbishing of a Nora Patrich/Juan Sanchos mural depicting the people of Vancouver East from a historic perspective. It had been in storage a long time and now is on permanent display at SFU so it can be enjoyed by the general public. I like this university's activism and the decentralized programs offered at its downtown campus.

NDP Activities

After I retired, I gradually eased out of NDP constituency activities. We were keen to replace the Liberal MP with a New Democrat in Vancouver East. I encouraged COPE City Councillor Libby Davies to run and helped her and her partner, Bruce Erickson, to move into Adanac Co-op to be in the riding. After Bruce died, Libby agreed to run and I worked hard for her. She won the nomination and went on to defeat Liberal Anna Terrana to become the MP for Vancouver East. She became an outstanding representative and parliamentarian. Glen Sanford, who had worked for me, was her able assistant and election organizer.

I continued to be a loyal NDP supporter, although like many New Democrats, I was saddened by our provincial failures and the internal conflicts that resulted in Glen Clark replacing Mike Harcourt as Premier. He was replaced by Ujjal Dosanjh in 2000, who was defeated in 2001. (He defected to the federal Liberals in 2003. New Democrats, including me, were disgusted when he won and became federal Minister of Health.) In the 2001 provincial election all but two NDP MLAs were defeated. The two women who won—Jenny Kwan and Joy McPhail—were from Vancouver East. Joy became a tough and courageous NDP leader. When Joy retired in 2003, Carole James was elected leader. Jenny became a mother, but continued the fight.

Federally we also struggled. Alexa McDonough eventually replaced Audrey McLaughlin as Leader of the federal NDP. She gained support for the NDP in the Maritimes, but we lost seats elsewhere. Svend Robinson and Libby Davies remained the only NDP MPs from BC. When Alexa resigned in 2002, Jack Layton, a Toronto City Councillor, was elected leader. I supported Jack early in his nomination campaign, feeling that he had the political smarts and the energy that the NDP needed.

In the June 2004 election the NDP won 19 seats. Ed Broadbent was returned to Parliament as Ottawa Centre MP, and Libby Davies retained her Vancouver East seat.

Vancouver's political left had a big boost when, in 2002, Mayor Larry Campbell and COPE won eight out of ten seats on Vancouver City Council. This was a major coup for the left that re-energized NDP members and involved many young people. We began to feel there was hope. However, by 2005, a major rift among the ten COPE council members split the group in half, and Jim Green formed a new Vision Vancouver party. We lost the majority in the Vancouver City election, including the Mayor's seat. Dark days were returning to City Hall.

CHAPTER 23

My Family

This chapter is written especially for my extended family. The story about Betty Speers is dedicated to her grandchildren.

If I were to characterize us four Learoyd siblings, we would be: the Missionary (Bill), the Socialist (Marg), the Capitalist (Ted), and the Hippie (Betty). We all came from conservative, middle-class, small-town Ontario, yet by the 1990s we represented a broad cross-section of Canadian society, with all its different lifestyles. Our extended clan in the next generation is also an interesting mix, and the 24 grandchildren (to date) are delightful.

In Memory of Betty Speers

I loved my sister Betty Speers, and Claude did, too. After he died and I retired, Betty and I spent more time together as companions and friends. We both loved adventure. She was a wonderfully relaxed person with a gentle manner and a good sense of humour. She was accepting of people and rarely judgmental. "Should" was not in her vocabulary. She believed people and the environment were one and must be respected (although she was less tolerant of would-be developers on her beloved Saturna Island).

We looked different, reflecting our different lifestyles. Betty was comfortably overweight with hair in a shiny bun or pigtail, usually wearing clothing from the Saturna Island Free Store. She smoked most of her life. I was a slimmer, white-haired, colour-coordinated, non-smoking urbanite. But underneath we shared the same values, which had been passed on to us by our parents—an interest in people and a belief in their capacities, a sense of humour and enjoyment of community, a zest for life (but always with an afternoon siesta), and a love of family with a respect for independence. Unlike our Alberta brothers, we both became New Democrats when we moved to BC. I became the wealthy socialist and she was poor, but it made no difference. She allowed me to treat for trips and she shared with me her fresh veggies and her children.

Betty's story reflects the courage, love and sense of adventure of a modern-day pioneer feminist. I include it as an example of an alternative lifestyle, and for her children to remember her by. In many ways, as the youngest sibling, Betty was a motherless child, what with our mother being hospitalized during four of Betty's preschool years. When Mother died, at age fifteen she became the chief housekeeper for Dad.

Betty's interest in farming started early when she stayed weekends with her surrogate mother on a local farm. Our father, the high-school principal, taught agriculture, and we always had large gardens and food to preserve during the Depression. Recycling was our way of life. Later, in war years, Betty was, like me, a Farmerette. In her teens, she had lots of pals to make mischief with. When she cut up in school, our dad used to say in disgust, "Some people's kids!"

Betty's interest in travel (and pubs) started early. When she was eight (and I was twelve), she and I travelled alone by bus to visit relatives in Chatham. We stopped to buy milk for our lunch at a beer parlour, much to the amusement of locals and the horror of our teetotaller parents.

After high school, Betty trained as a nurse, a very tough training in those days. She maintained a lifelong friendship with fellow graduates. She took a job in Winnipeg, married Jack Speers, and they moved to Edmonton, where Jane and David were born. Those were tough times, with the family living in a basement suite and struggling to make ends meet in the freezing-cold weather. After a spring visit to Vancouver where the rhododendrons were blooming, the family decided to move to Richmond, BC, where Ken and Tracy joined their family. Many other Richmond kids hung out at the Speers' home as they were growing up.

Betty became increasingly concerned about the rigidity of the education system in Richmond, and turned to alternative schools. Ken and David were enrolled in the new Saturna Island Free School (based on the Summerhill model). The children took the ferry to the Island, spent several days at the school, then several days at home.

Betty liked the school's concept of free expression and creative development, but the boys were less enthusiastic. After two years, they returned to the Richmond school system. Betty then decided to "change the system from within," and became an elected school trustee for two years. Jack taught in Burnaby. The Speers home became a centre for troubled teenagers. Later, their extended family included Debby Foisy (singer-songwriter Ferron) and Cathy Goldney.

Since Betty and Jack owned shares in the Saturna Island property, which had become Breezy Bay Farm, the family used it for summer holidays, eventually building a cabin on the side of the mountain. Because of a lack of funds and a commitment to conservation, they lived a simple life. The cabin was built from recycled building materials. The family slept on "foamies" in a loft, and the outhouse was out back. They had no electricity for many years, and water was carried from a nearby well. But the wood stove worked well, and they used lots of ingenuity. Betty got into organic gardening and raised organic chickens to feed the family.

At age 50, Betty decided to leave Jack and face the future on her own—a frightening prospect for someone with no savings, no income, and no recent work history. She stayed with Claude and me while retraining as a nurse and working at Burnaby Hospital. However, Betty was not happy in traditional hospital nursing. She objected to the routine sedation and restraint of elderly patients, and would surreptitiously free them when she could. A part-time job in group homes in Vancouver soon replaced hospital work. Saturna was now her home.

In 1978 Betty and her friend Dawne Milligan decided to share the Saturna Island cabin and give up their town jobs. For a while, Dawne taught school as well as piano, while Betty worked on a training grant learning to use computers for bookkeeping. (Thereafter she became the treasurer for almost every group on the island.) Dawne, who suffered from many allergies, eventually moved back to town, but she and Betty remained very close friends.

Betty became even more active in the Breezy Bay Farm. She started organic gardening in earnest, and built a greenhouse from recycled materials. Her tomatoes and salad greens were delicious and soon in demand on Saturna. Together, the co-operative community that makes up the farm rehabilitated a century-old farmhouse and developed it as a bed-and-breakfast, providing summer employment.

Betty was also active in the larger community. In fact, she was so active in the Community Club, the Health Committee, the Recycling Project, the Library, and the Women's Group that I started to call her "the Mayor of Saturna."

In summer, Betty's children and grandchildren (now totalling ten) often visited her—or "Grandma Chicken" as they called her in tribute to her poultry-raising prowess—and Betty encouraged their love of nature and creative projects. The cousins enjoyed the freedom of the farm, exploring the duck pond and the beach and hiking the cliffs. In winter we had clan gatherings at our place on Mayne Island, which was larger and heated. We held Betty's 70th birthday party there, which she called "a blast."

Betty and I did a lot of island-hopping to get together on either Mayne or Saturna, so in 2001 I decided to look for a place on Saturna and sell my home on Mayne. Eventually Betty suggested that I extend her cabin and share with her instead of buying a house. We began making plans with Chuck, the builder.

I had always assumed, since I was four years older, that I would die first, so I had put most of my assets in our joint names. This gave us a fund to get the building started. We designed the extension on the hillside cabin to have an upstairs and a downstairs, with a large room and bathroom on each floor—the upper room for me and the lower for family—as well as laundry facilities in the lower level.

Although this was contrary to Betty's minimalist lifestyle, she helped to plan the extension. She joked about it later, saying, "Imagine my humiliation when two bathrooms and a dishwasher and a modern kitchen were added!" An attractive wraparound veranda joined the two wings. We kept the shingled rear walls of the cabin as they were, for contrast. We conformed to environmental needs for Dawne's allergies, and Tracy and Celine took over the annex that Dawne's father had built. A well was drilled and roads were improved.

After moving some furniture from Mayne, I put my Mayne house up for sale. During the next year, I learned that there was no occupancy permit and that several repairs were needed. My good friend Geoff Cue, from Salt Spring Island, came to the rescue to do most of them. But even he couldn't move the house back ten metres from the property line, so this error was grandfathered and forgiven.

I now spent considerable time on Saturna and joined Betty in many of her activities—a women's group, Breezy Bay management meetings, Celine's fun, and community events, including the hugely successful Saturna Lamb Barbecue, an annual event that draws boats and hundreds of visitors from surrounding islands, and which has for years financed the community hall. Betty specialized in "Betty's Greens," which she grew for the nearby Saturna Lodge.

In the spring of 2001 Betty fainted at a nurses' reunion she was attending in Edmonton. Her friends sent her to hospital for a check-up, but there appeared to be no problem. Late the next fall she received a report from the Edmonton Hospital with x-rays showing a small growth on her lung. The Victoria Hospital confirmed it was lung cancer. Although she had given it up a few years before this, Betty had smoked for most of her life.

Betty's children were very concerned, and Dawne Milligan researched resources and alternative treatments. Betty went into hospital in Victoria for an operation to remove the tumour. I stayed in Victoria with Marjorie Martin for two weeks and visited Betty. She was told it was serious.

Eventually when Betty was ready to go home, we decided that she would be better off in Vancouver, close to medical services and care. I drove her over on the ferry in her wheelchair and settled her into my large en suite bedroom. I rented a lounge chair for the front window, and from there she enjoyed the view of False Creek activities.

Family and friends visited often and Bill Sheffeld, her executor, helped her with her will. Her son David and his wife Sue brought their three boys to visit or to entertain their grandma on the ground outside her window. Her daughter Tracy came over on her days off from working at the Lodge. Her son Ken visited twice from Parksville. When our brother Bill came from Alberta, and daughter Jane came from Ontario, I slept at my neighbour Irene's condo.

Dawne and Claudia Macdonald were regular visitors and advisors. Love poured over from Saturna through many visitors and was clearly expressed in a front-page photo in the Island Tides newspaper. In it, a smiling crowd of Saturna Island residents holds a banner which reads, "We love you, Betty."

Finally, with Betty's help, her family began to accept that she was dying. It was their first experience with death and very upsetting. Betty and I, being older, accepted that dying was part of living and that it was inevitable. But it wasn't easy. Once again, I had difficulty expressing my feelings.

Betty was in palliative care at Vancouver General Hospital for awhile and then came home again to my apartment. Visits from community nurses and homemakers were very helpful. Morphine deadened the pain, but she was eating very little. Given my bad back, I eventually found it difficult to move Betty and one evening could not get her into her bed. In desperation, I called medical resources, who were no help. Finally, I called 9-1-1. Two big, handsome firefighters came to the rescue and lifted her from the floor to her bed.

We realized I could no longer cope, so Betty was moved to the Cottage Hospice in Vancouver East. It is a loving, family-oriented palliative care centre in a park area. For her last weeks, Betty enjoyed many visitors. Dawne visited each morning. Betty Jardine from Breezy Bay Farm stayed with her overnight, and so did I. David and Sue were with her on the night she died. The next morning, David put an eagle feather in her hair. She looked like a warrior at peace.

Several weeks after Betty died, we held a celebration of her life at Breezy Bay Farm. It was a lovely spring day, and many folks gathered in the orchard or on the winding veranda of the lovely old farmhouse, now a bed-and-breakfast. Grandchildren darted about. Jacqui Campbell from Saturna was MC, and most of the family spoke, as did Betty's friends. It was a love-in. Gord Kristjensen, in typical Saturna style, had organized music, and Tracy had arranged for food. A lone eagle soared, then dipped down, seemingly in salute.

The following summer we held a family gathering on the high hillside overlooking Plumper Sound to dedicate "Betty's Bench" and spread her ashes. Betty's long-time friend, Corrine Moffit, represented her nursing friends who had donated the bench. Jane and her family also came west for the occasion.

Ken had built a cement base for the bench. He added a mound where Betty's ten grandchildren left their handprints and names, and Jane added a birdhouse. We felt very close to Breezy Bay residents who also had been Betty's family, including Betty Jardine, Bill and Kathy Sheffeld, Reni and Bakhshish, and the three House families. (Marjorie Cohen and Michael Goldrick, who had become recent friends, were away). We enjoyed the serene surroundings and thought of Betty. Once again an eagle flew overhead.

One of Betty's greatest gifts to me was sharing her kids and her ten beloved grandchildren. During the last months when she stayed with me in Vancouver, we had many wonderful times together. She was peaceful and surrounded by the love of her family and her many friends. Her spirit lives on. . . .

The Next Generation

I loved kids, but was unable to have any after the ovarian cancer in 1957. I had watched Betty's four handsome children grow, and eventually have children of their own. Looking back, I can see I was following in the roles of my own aunts—Hilda and Alma—by participating in family fun and providing financial help when needed. I didn't see a lot of my nieces and nephews while I was working, but we all enjoyed get-togethers at our trailer on Welbury Point on Salt Spring Island, and later at our place on Mayne Island. I now enjoy our extended family—the Speers, Learoyds, Mitchells and Miltons. I was the closest to the Speers (Betty and Jack) family, since they lived nearby in Richmond.

Betty and Jack had four children—Jane, David, Ken, and Tracy (who was adopted). David married Sue. In addition to their three boys—Derek, Justin and Travis—Sue's niece Katie joined them. The boys grew tall and challenged their father on the soccer field. David now has a house-moving business. He often drops by to joke and check up on me.

Betty's oldest child, Jane, lives in Tillsonburg, Ontario and we see her less often. She married Richard Shepherd and they have two children—Cody and Laura. Jane works as a receptionist and is the main breadwinner. Richard was injured working in the Alberta gas fields and eventually became a stay-at-home dad. He has helped Cody become a champion hockey player.

Ken Speers married Kelly and they have three daughters—Mariah, Coral, and Shaye. Ken has developed a successful cement business in Parksville on Vancouver Island, and Kelly works for a travel agency.

Despite the stresses of raising two daughters (Jenna and Celine) as a single mom, Tracy overcame many adversities. She moved from Saturna Island to Vancouver and now manages a restaurant. She and Celine live near me and often drop in to help. I enjoy their visits.

The Learoyds

My oldest brother, Bill Learoyd, and his wife, Nadine, were bilingual missionaries in Montreal for many years. (Betty and I were relieved when Bill stopped trying to convert us.) Bill and Nadine adopted two boys, Luc and Bobby. When Bill retired, they moved to Three Hills, Alberta. Later, Luc returned home to help when Nadine developed Parkinson's disease, and eventually died.

My younger brother, Ted Learoyd, married Kay Leggatt. They moved from Chatham, Ontario to Calgary, where Ted held a senior position in a gas company. Their five children—Sue, Jeff, Carol, Brian, and Pete—all went to college or university. Sue settled in Ottawa and co-ordinates CUSO workers in Africa. The four younger children have produced thirteen grandchildren. (Kay finally won the competition with Betty.) After Ted died of cancer in 1993, Betty and I welcomed Kay as our third sister for our travels.

After Betty died, I developed a close family relationship with my cousin Liz Milton and her two children. Liz lives in Victoria and since her retirement has become an artist. Her two kids—Lex and Cynthia—now live in Montréal.

Claude's brother, Des Mitchell, his wife, Ann, and their three children, Bill, Patti-Ann, and Jennifer, moved to California after he retired. Their teenage kids grew up on a lovely ranch. We have maintained a fond relationship but I have rarely seen them since both Des and Claude died.

CHAPTER 24

Travel Tales

Travel has always been important in my life. As a child I routinely travelled back and forth to kindergarten, to visit my aunts, and to visit my mother in hospital. As I got older, I went away to camp, to work, and to school. I jumped at the opportunity to work with the Red Cross in Japan and Korea. A good part of my interest in working with refugees overseas was the opportunity it afforded me to see other parts of the world, and many of my friendships have been forged around travel. And certainly my relationship with Claude was bound up in our mutual interest in people and exploring different cultures and ways of life.

While I was a Member of Parliament, I enjoyed the opportunities I had to travel to different conferences and events both in Canada and internationally, meeting other parliamentarians and social activists. That interest continued after my retirement, and fortunately I was able to travel extensively. I was in good health, had no responsibilities, and was financially secure.

Mexico with Audrey

On one occasion I accompanied Audrey McLaughlin to Mexico, a country I had visited frequently with Claude. But this was 1996, and we were visiting Chiapas, where uprisings of Zapatista rebels were causing the government concern. Both Audrey and I were interested in the revolution taking place in the area. Through her government contacts, we were assigned a car, a driver, an interpreter, and a (conservative) Mexican MP to escort us. We managed to escape all of their surveillance to meet with "lefties" in San Cristobal, and enjoyed getting together with the collective at an environmental centre.

Later our government hosts drove us into the mountains where Mayan ruins had only recently been reclaimed from the jungle. We stayed at a luxurious jungle "retreat" and were flown by helicopter over the ruins. On our return we were stopped by a Zapatista roadblock. Audrey and I in our hearts wanted to join the "rebels," but were obliged to remain quietly with our conservative chaperone. Eventually our hosts bade us fond farewell, after refusing to allow us to pay any of our expenses.

I visited Cuba twice. On my first visit, in the '80s, Claude and I travelled with a French-speaking group from Quebec. A decade later, Patsy George and I travelled to Havana, where we met with a number of Cubans who seemed fairly satisfied with the Castro regime.

Usually my sister Betty was my travel companion, though occasionally we were joined by Audrey or Kay Learoyd. Our travels took us in a lot of different directions. Betty and I explored St. Lucia and Barbados, and took a Panama Canal cruise with Kay and Bessie Lee, and we jumped ship for a jungle safari in Costa Rica. On one occasion we drove to the Yukon to visit Audrey. But it was our trip to South Asia that left us with some of our most memorable moments.

South Asia with Betty and Audrey

Betty and I planned a trip to Thailand, India and Nepal in 1993. Audrey came with us. She was feeling down after the recent NDP election losses. In several airports, Canadians of Indian origin came up to greet her warmly. She finally said with a laugh, "I have more votes here than I got in Canada."

We arrived in Bangkok on Christmas Eve. After a traumatic trip in the noisy traffic, we suffered through a boring and tasteless traditional North American Christmas dinner at our hotel. The next day our charming guide took us by boat to see the city and visit Buddhist temples. Thai people are proud monarchists and deeply religious. We were careful to respect their traditions, although I was almost thrown out of one temple for wearing sandals with bare heels. In the afternoon our guide invited us to her home for tea, and we met her sisters and mother, who were tending their store.

By the time we had received many floral tributes and visited many temples, I was laughingly designated the "high priestess" of our group. I accepted this honour graciously and demanded respect whenever I could get away with it. My status was confirmed when I raised my arms and the heavy traffic stopped, when I was given preference for a bump-up to first class at the airport, and when I was bitten by a monkey and recovered.

The monkey incident happened on our trip north. We left Bangkok in the early morning, travelling by car, canoe and elephant. Our guide, John, had spent time in Prince George, BC, and promised to give us a "number one" tour. After a ride up the river in a Thai canoe, we were introduced to our elephants. We climbed up a high stand to reach their backs, two per elephant, and were told to hold on tightly to the primitive wooden seat. It was difficult to stay seated as the elephant plunged down hills, crossed ravines, and crashed through forests.

We were stiff, cold, and exhausted when we arrived in Chiang Mai. Betty said, "What we need now is a Thai massage to soothe our battered bodies and warm us up." Betty had been told in Canada that the Thais did a wonderful massage. We saw a massage parlour sign, but John was reluctant to take us there. However we insisted this would cure our ills.

We were shown in the back entrance, were each given a giggling masseuse, and the torture began. Bend, pull, thump, twist! Audrey shouted, "Watch my sprained ankle." John translated. Betty demanded they avoid her injured hip and I fiercely protected my vulnerable neck. John duly translated while enjoying his own massage. We moaned and groaned but agreed that at least we were warm now.

After the massage I visited the toilet, which had no light. To my horror, my wallet containing money and tickets dropped down the hole. In disgust I fished it out. As we were leaving, enthusiastic male customers were arriving. We finally realized we were in a brothel. To add to our misery, that night we were lodged in a cramped, dark, damp room. Audrey, who always preferred a single room, was sandwiched between two snorers with a single blanket to cover her. A stiff drink of scotch helped to console us.

The next day we drove to the Chiang Mai border and gazed at the three converging countries—Laos, Thailand, and Myanmar—which form the "Golden Triangle," famous for drug trafficking and prostitution, and once a popular destination for soldiers on leave from the Vietnam War. In the background the Chinese hills loomed. We tried to cross the border into Myanmar (formerly Burma) but were stopped by border guards.

On our return trip to Bangkok we visited caves that were guarded by monkeys. When I bent to pick up peanuts to feed them to one monkey, he attacked me ferociously, biting me twice on the knee. Betty, fearing rabies, consulted a doctor, who said we would know in ten days if the monkey was infected. If it was, I would be a goner. There was no cure for rabies, we were told.

Since we were leaving for India the next day, we arranged with John to check on the health of the monkey. He was to phone us in India each day to report. For ten days our Indian tourist agency received strange messages. "Monkey not sick." "Monkey OK today." After the tenth day, when the monkey was pronounced healthy, we relaxed. I was not going to die of rabies after all. We could continue our travels around India and Nepal.

On to India

We spent our first few days in India in Mumbai (formerly Bombay). We travelled through overwhelming crowds to visit the home of Mahatma Gandhi. Reading original manuscripts, we became immersed in the amazing revolution he had led to free India from British domination by non-violent means.

Another memorable experience in Mumbai was a ferry trip to the popular Elephant Caves, located on an island. The boat was so overcrowded that we were sure it would capsize. When it finally arrived safely, scores of impatient returning passengers nearly pushed us overboard while trying to board the boat.

My friend Crissy George, who was visiting her family in Cochin, South India, met us there in a comfortable, cool hotel. She had arranged our itinerary with her brother, Lancy George, who runs a tourist agency. (Taking monkey-health calls was not their usual service.) We absorbed the sights and sounds and smells of South India. Kerala is a Marxist state that holds democratic elections. Its progressive policies are reflected in the 98-percent literacy rate, land reforms, progressive labour policies, and successful family planning. However, we noted that, although forbidden by law, the caste system and dowry practices still existed in subtler forms.

We visited a women's co-operative workshop, which Monsignor Payapilly (called "Father" by Crissy) helped to establish. He is a long-time friend of her family who had visited my cottage on Mayne Island when he was in Canada. The workshop enabled illiterate women to develop skills and earn a small income. He also was helping rural women to survive by giving each a goat with which to feed her family and reproduce goats for sale. We brought with us a generous cheque from Margaret Motz (a Canadian friend of Patsy's) for goat purchases.

"Father" receded into the background when we reached the Bishop's palace. The Bishop reigned supreme and received the cheque for the goats. We were treated to wine and a sumptuous meal. Red and gold were everywhere. Afterwards, the self-righteous Bishop took us to his office and personally signed a large photo of himself for each of us. (Mine became a mock shrine in my hotel room.) I felt that the women who lived in such poverty (and not the Bishop) should have been getting the recognition for their efforts.

It was a long drive back in the sweltering tropical heat. I wondered why Crissy insisted I sit in the middle of the front seat, where the sun poured in. "Father" cringed away from me into the door while I sweated in my short dress next to Lancy, the driver. The heat was unbearable. (Later Crissy told me that it was taboo for her, a parishioner and Indian woman, to sit between the men, but it was okay for me.)

Audrey's fame had spread, and she was sometimes referred to as Canada's Prime Minister. When Lancy took us to meet a retired politician, we were welcomed for tea. As we entered, Audrey tripped and fell at his feet. Not to be outdone, as we were leaving I leaned on a fragile table and crashed tea cups to the floor. Our host's wife, who was English, met us the next day and said, "I hear you had a smashing tea party." Despite this incident Audrey did us proud when she spoke to a men's group, dressed in her colourful new Indian sari.

Lancy had arranged a trip for us through the backwaters, a complex network of lagoons, lakes and canals. Audrey was escorted aboard a large boat with her three handmaidens. Crissy explained that peasants living on the floating islands were following the age-old tradition of their caste.

Our trip also included a stay at two lovely resorts. One evening on a river jungle cruise we saw herds of elephants on the shore. Baited by passengers, the bull elephant tried to attack our boat. Driving back to Cochin we saw tea plantations with unionized women workers, rubber trees being tapped, and glorious flowers everywhere.

Lancy and his wife and daughter were wonderful hosts. He is the youngest child, with five older sisters. He inherited the family home and land but sold it to build a lovely city home with a garden. They took us to see the classical dance drama of Kerala, called Kathakali. Another day we visited the oldest synagogue in India. When it was time to leave, we flew north to Delhi, where it was cold and wet. People were sleeping on the roadsides with a wet blanket for cover.

In Delhi we went shopping for gifts to take home. At a carpet store we enjoyed a dramatic performance by one rug merchant, who had his minions display an assortment of his wares. When he saw a twinkle in my eye he said, "Madam, this carpet is made by a women's co-operative from the finest of wool that was taken from the underbelly of newborn lambs that have never seen the light of day." Who could resist such salesmanship? Needless to say, I bought it.

The Taj Mahal, commemorating one of the world's great love stories, was as beautiful as any pictures of it I had seen. Audrey and I took an overnight trip to visit Jaipur in Rajasthan state while Betty rested. We rode glamorously decorated elephants and were taken to the tourist spots. Tiring of commercialism, we told our overprotective guide that we wanted free time in the evening. We escaped for a luxurious dinner at the Maharaja's palace. Afterward, a fantastic wedding party arrived with drums beating, traditional music, and decorated elephants. I was fascinated by the elaborate pomp and ceremony.

As we drove to the airport to leave Delhi, the faces of children begging for money appeared at the car window at every stop. Families sleeping under bridges hung their clothes on fences to dry. I realized how insulated we had been from the real India.

Trekking in Nepal

En route home we stayed in a hostel in Kathmandu, along with many other travellers and trekkers. Government workers stayed in luxury hotels nearby. We wandered the winding streets, visiting shops and tea houses that catered to tourists.

Aid workers we had met in Canada introduced us to several Nepalese. One was a retired worker who took us to his village, entertained us to tea with his family on the rooftop of their home, and showed us local points of interest. Another contact was with a woman named Rana (whose name indicated she was connected to the royal family). She drove us up a local mountain from which we could view Mount Everest.

Most interesting was our visit and discussion with the former leader of the Congress Party of Nepal, who had led the recent revolution to democratize the country. He had been a political exile in India for many years. His wife, an outstanding woman, had led an underground women's movement in rural Nepal. When we met them they were both elderly, but were interested that we were fellow democratic socialists from Canada. We were served tea in their lovely garden.

When Audrey left for home, Betty and I headed north, where tourists and trekkers congregated. The old bus to Pokhara was jammed with people. It crawled up the steep, narrow mountain roads, clinging to the left-hand side while we cringed at the sheer drop on the right. When we met an oncoming bus there was no room to pass in the single lane. The drivers consulted for a long time. Finally, in fear and trepidation, we managed to squeeze past the other bus, avoiding what looked like an imminent landslide.

Pokhara is a lovely tourist town and we relaxed in a hotel near the lake. We became friends with a young couple who told us all about trekking. We were so intrigued that we decided we could not be so close to Mount Everest and not try it ourselves.

One morning we headed upward with two teenagers who insisted on being our guides. After the first stretch of hiking, we stopped at a tiny hut on the mountainside that sold drinks. Inside the dark hut we sat with a mother who was caring for her sick child. It looked a dismal life. Despite our enthusiasm for the idea, we soon realized that trekking days were over for us two seniors. Our young guides left us in disgust after taking us down hills (going down was worse than going up) and across rice fields to a boat, which, thankfully, eventually deposited us at our hotel.

Return to India: The Kindness of Strangers

I returned to India in 1994 to attend a meeting of the Socialist International Women, chaired by Audrey McLaughlin. After the conference I flew to Varanasi (formerly Benares), the holy city of the Hindus, where "Mother Ganges meets the sky" and brings enlightenment to people who bathe in her waters. This stands out as the high point of my time in India. The impact of this experience continues to stay with me.

I was greeted at the airport by Anil Kishnan ("Chris"), a very knowledgeable and considerate guide. As we drove on, we became submerged in a sea of people, cattle, rickshaws, honking taxis, and much activity. The muddy streets, primitive housing, roadside markets, and narrow back lanes were reminders that this was the oldest city in India.

We drove through busy streets to a silk factory owned by Muslims. Although in the minority, Muslims have considerable influence because they control major industries and hire only Muslims. Five old men sat in the sun outside the factory. I followed Chris down narrow, dark alleys to a room where several men and boys were weaving beautiful silk. One man, who was very thin, worked long hours with only one day off a year, I heard. His father had been a weaver, as is his ten-year-old son. A raised platform with a TV set on it was apparently where they lived. I asked Chris where the women were. He explained that as Muslims, they worked behind screens and did not go out in public. The manager showed me beautiful silks and I bought some to make into valance curtains.

I woke early the next morning in order to be on a boat on the Ganges at sunrise. We drove through crowds of pilgrims who had come from afar to worship at the holy river. As we walked to the river, slipping in dung, we were pressed by the thickening crowds, bicycles, carts, and motorcycles. Chris had arranged for a boat rowed by a young boy. It was still dark when we started our journey up the river.

Suddenly I realized my money belt was gone! Gone also were my passport, travellers cheques, credit cards, rupees, and dollars. Everything! I could not even pay for the floating candles or oarsman.

I started to panic. Chris calmed me down by suggesting I may have left my purse in the car. With difficulty I postponed the crisis to continue the tour.

Out on the water, Chris described the historical significance of the many ghats (steps and temples) that lined the riverbank. Many had been built by kings from across India. Dawn broke, and a glorious red globe rose from the horizon, silhouetting boats and people. Thousands of pilgrims bathed in the river and collected samples of holy water. Others prayed with priests or meditated on shelves above the steps. An animal carcass floated by. We passed the cremation ghat, where bodies must be burned the day of death. Bottles of ashes hung from trees, waiting to be thrown in the Ganges for eternal life.

Chris paid the oarsman and we started the search for our car through narrow lanes of the bazaar, elbowing our way through dense streams of people and sacred cows. My panic was escalating rapidly. What would I do for money? Finally we found our car and driver. But no purse! Chris agreed that if the purse was stolen or lost in the crowd we would never find it. He very kindly offered to buy my ticket back to Delhi.

We went back to the hotel and I tried to phone Audrey in Delhi for emergency funds. There was no answer. Although a seasoned traveller, I had never before been stranded without funds. Always I had separated monies for emergencies. But not this time. Chris and I sat in silent desperation, wondering what to do next.

A phone rang and a hotel employee wandered over to speak to Chris. Imagine our joy when we were told that the call had come from the police and that they had my purse! We immediately headed for the police station. The policeman asked me to check my wallet. To my great relief, all was intact. I tried to give the policeman a gift. He politely refused saying, "It is our duty, Madam." We went on another tour of the ghetto to find the storekeeper who had turned in my purse. He explained that a friend had seen me drop the purse and had brought it to his shop. They found the travel bureau address and then took it to the police. I thanked everyone and tried to pay a reward to each person. All refused, saying, "No, it is our duty."

I marvelled at the ethics of people who could have kept enough money to feed their families for a year. In the poorest city in one of the poorest countries in the world, such generosity and respect was amazing. Was it the Hindu religion that spawned such honesty? Whatever the motive, I would retell this story many times. Each time it restored my faith in human nature.

Middle East

In 1996 sister Betty, sister-in-law Kay, and I joined an Elder Hostel tour in Greece. We enjoyed an educational commentary as we visited ancient sites. While shopping one day, Betty tripped and fell, injuring her leg. She would have to get around on crutches for the rest of the trip.

We continued the second week of the tour on the Elder Hostel boat, enjoying Greek food and visits to Greek Islands. Betty stayed on board, entertaining the Greek crew. We had travelled on my travel points, and when we returned to Athens, I panicked because we were barely able to get together enough money to fly home. Our plans to visit Israel had to be postponed.

In the fall of 1998, Betty and I spent seven weeks in the Middle East. We made our own arrangements, staying in guest-houses in Turkey and at hostels for pilgrims in Israel. Egypt seemed more intimidating, so we joined a tour there after a short stop in Jordan. Here is Betty's account of those travels.

Turkey

Six days in Istanbul introduced us to a Muslim way of life—awakening to prayer calls from the nearby Blue Mosque, dressing conservatively (especially hard for Marg), visiting the markets and mosques, or just roaming about absorbing the sights, sounds, and heat.

After orientation in Istanbul, we bused all night to central Turkey—the Cappadocia region. There we toured fascinating sand hills, caves and four-level cave communities where the Crusaders had lived underground. Our guide was raised in a cave.

Another luxury bus, complete with steward and amenities, took us by day through the plateaus and irrigated valleys featuring potatoes in the central area and cotton in the south to Anatalya on the Mediterranean. We settled into a guest-house in the old city with a courtyard garden of orange trees.

One night we caught a free bus at the statue of Ataturk to Aspendos, where we heard the Vienna Symphony play in a 1000-year-old amphitheatre lit only by candle as the full moon rose over the ramparts above the orchestra. Unforgettable.

Since neither of us are sunbathers, the resorts we stayed in along the Aegean coast were restful, but not as interesting. Our final visit was to the ancient city of Ephesus, which was rebuilt by Alexander the Great in 334 BC, covered by silt from earthquakes and floods, and reclaimed by Turks in this century. The huge amphitheatre (which was shaken recently by rock concerts), the 'love rooms', the latrines, and the elaborate library were impressive.

Israel

We flew from Ismar airport to Tel Aviv on October 11 where we met Crissy and Patsy George, Margaret Motz, and Fred Molowski. After the holiday weekend, we rented a van and drove up the coast, across to the Sea of Galilee and down to Jerusalem, Bethlehem, Masada and back to the old city of Jerusalem for another week.

After the very modern city of Tel Aviv, the old cities of Jaffa and Haifa took us back to the past. We roamed the subterranean maze of streets in the walled city of Akka while lively children followed, pretending to take our photo. We stayed two nights in Tiberias on the Sea of Galilee and from there drove up the Golan Heights where Syrian and Israeli settlers both want land and security. Crossing the Jordan River, now a small creek, and visiting Bethlehem (where the manger is a small cave under a church) brought back many biblical memories.

Marg had arranged with an Israeli woman she had met in Vancouver to spend time on her kibbutz. Ester took us to the factory, farm, daycare, and seniors' sites and explained the difficulty they had supporting all the services and agreeing on how to share their incomes, cars, and travel allowances. With the young people wanting to explore the world or just leave home, the decisions are difficult.

Before returning the van we visited the ancient Masada fortress south of Jerusalem on a desert mountain where Jews fought the Romans until they all were killed. We did not swim or float in the nearby Dead Sea, nor did we buy the wonderful rejuvenating lotions sold at the En Gedi Spa.

We stayed in an evangelical Anglican hostel at the Jaffa Gate in old Jerusalem. Patsy smuggled Fred into her room despite the prohibitions, and we roamed the ancient markets of the old city. Orthodox Jewish men were everywhere wearing their black suits, top hats, side curls, beards and prayer shawls. On a walking tour through the Armenian section, Margaret learned about the genocide of one million Armenians by the Turks. The Arab section was larger but poorer than the Jewish section, which had been rebuilt on a bombed-out area, preserving ancient buildings below ground level. Bar mitzvahs were performed at the Wailing Wall where men and women prayed separately. Christian shrines were full of pilgrims. A split rock was believed to be caused by Christ's tomb, dripping blood. I [Betty] rested and roamed through the old souk (market) but was no match bargaining with the Arab shopkeepers.

The high point of Jerusalem was a half-day spent with former Vancouver colleague Devora (Donna) Levin and her friends. Abrihim lives in the old city and is an artist. He started a craft co-op to enable Ethiopian women to earn a livelihood and has a delightful room for a B&B. Eric and his wife served us tea in a modern condo built by Canadian architect Moshe Safdie. Hannah's old house on the former Israel-Jordan border had been bombed while she and her young son hid in the basement. She, too, is a marvellous artist. We also met a Palestinian friend of Arafat who runs a café. He predicted there will be open warfare by 2000 between Jews and Palestinians.

We did a circle tour of the city, passing the King David Hotel, new communities, and the Mount of Olives en route to the Holocaust Museum. Hundreds of dead children were named and remembered with a star in the dark Children's Museum.

Jordan

Margaret and I found the main bus depot in Jerusalem and climbed aboard a bus, expecting to go through Hebron on the way to Eilat. The bus station had many young people in uniform with guns casually slung over their shoulders, heading out of the city. We were dropped off the bus near the Jordanian border crossing. We struggled in extreme heat, walking with all the luggage the half mile to Aqaba customs.

An aggressive Jordanian taxi driver captured our bedraggled duo after we paid an exorbitant Canadian visa fee. He took us to a back-street hotel in Aqaba and the next day drove us to Petra, where we stayed in his uncle's hotel (Cleo Petra by name). As we drove we noted there is little agriculture in south Jordan—just a few greenhouses, fields for winter crops for sheep, and sand, sand, sand.

At the Hotel Cleo Petra we joined Arab men in the lobby to watch TV. King Hussein, "the Little King," had been undergoing cancer treatment in the US and had come out of hospital to help with peace talks between Palestinians and Israelis. The Arab men around us watched with pride as King Hussein was praised by President Bill Clinton for breaking the impasse in the peace talks.

The next day we bounced in a donkey cart through a dry gorge to the ancient rock city of Petra. Buildings, such as the Treasury, homes, and an amphitheatre had been carved from beautiful reddish rock many eons ago. Workers were still excavating areas. Bedouins operate all businesses.

Egypt

On October 25 we took a modern jet ferry across the Gulf of Aqaba to Neweiba in Egypt on the coast of the Sinai Desert. The taxi driver took us to a beach hostel where most of the grass huts were empty of students—just us and the noisy camels peering in our window. Tramping the beach and lazing in the grass gazebo listening to punk music and the waves prepared us for the next journey across the Sinai Desert to Cairo.

Cairo was the place where Marg reached her glory as a bargainer. She was armed with the figure of 10 Egyptian Pounds (P) for a taxi to our hotel. So when the gates opened after we were off the bus, and fifty drivers swarmed around us looking for a steep fare from unsuspecting Anglos, she was ready. She so valiantly stuck to her terms and ridiculed their insistence that a reasonable fare would be 20P that we were left stranded by all the drivers. Then, just as I was beginning to lose confidence in her, a lone cab arrived and she quickly boosted the offer to 15P. That got us to our hotel, where we joined our tour. After five weeks as our own tour guides, it was a relief to relax and be organized by our Australian guide from Imaginative Travel.

"Antiquity" went back several thousand years. We crawled down the four-foot high tunnel under the pyramid to see the empty crypt fifty feet below ground. It is no place to have a heart attack. The nearby sphinx left us rather cold. Cairo Museum is first-rate. Young King Tut's treasures are the only ones left, as grave robbers had pillaged the other tombs.

A sleeper train to Aswan saved a hotel bill and was comfortable. I was up at sunrise and watched the richly irrigated fields along the Nile backed by the hills of the desert. The realization that there really is NO rain in Egypt is mind-boggling. Terrorist assassinations of tourists have curtailed jobs and tourist business.

Marg had had one desire in going to Egypt: to sail on a felucca, the ancient sailing ship of Egypt. She got her wish, as well as a chance to slide down the dunes to the Nile and see a light show at Isis ruins.

. . .

A visit to a Nubian village on an island in the Nile (one of the places where Nubian people were sent when the Aswan dam flooded their land) took place at night. Village men played African drums and everyone but me (Betty) danced on their boat. We climbed up sand hills to the village by moonlight to be served a Nubian feast by the men in a courtyard of one of the many no-roofed houses. Afterward women came with their crafts and tattooing while the men smoked hookah water pipes. A long, memorable day.

After another water journey on SS Amy (thirty people) we went inland to a camel auction where hundreds of camels were awaiting sale with one leg tied at the knee (hobbled, thank goodness). The temple at Edfu was the last stop before we moored at Luxor.

The adventure part of this trip was to be a half-day donkey ride to the Valley of the Kings—and it was. At the second stop when Marg tried mounting independently, the saddle slipped and she smacked her head on the pavement. Luckily her packsack broke the fall a bit and the goose-egged head seemed to be the only injury. (Perhaps her memory cells lost a bit, too.) We completed the long hot ride to the tombs that had been cleared of all treasures but had intact wall paintings. The longer a king lived, the longer the painted passage to the empty tomb. After some last-minute shopping at the souk, we left on an overnight train back to Cairo. A farewell dinner with the Aussies and Akemi, our Japanese friend, ended the tour.

. . .

Getting out of town was another matter. Only a late-night flight was available from Cairo to Tel Aviv. Connections were crucial. When we got to the head of the line after several hours wait the officials informed me, "There is a small problem, madam—your ticket is cancelled." A furious blast emitted from Marg's usually calm sister, who shrieked, "This is no problem—this is a catastrophe! If you don't get me on that plane I will lie down on the floor of this airport until you do!" They found me a seat. We sat out the night in the Israeli airport, under tight security.

At the Penn Club in London for an overnight rest, I fell asleep in the lobby while Marg was told we had no booking. In her delicate and persuasive manner she got us a room. The next day we took a lovely trip on a double-decker bus which wound its way to the airport, and then we were off for home.

Longboating in the UK

In 1999 Nora Curry and I, along with Geoff and Doreen Cue, shared a longboat up the Severn Canal to Stratford-on-Avon in the UK. The Captain (Geoff) had been ill and his three elderly crew lacked a certain strength and spryness required to leap off the boat to shore and open the ancient locks. It was not the most speedy or joyful of cruises. We saw my niece Carol and her four kids in Bristol. Afterward Nora and I went to Ireland. She introduced me to her friends and we had a wonderful night of pub music in Dublin, followed by a trip to Canamara, before we left for home.

Down Under

In 2000 I returned to Australia and New Zealand, accompanied by Audrey McLaughlin, and took the opportunity to get together with old friends. On the Gold Coast I visited my old Salt Spring Island pal, Walter Mailey, and his new wife, Dorothy, and stayed in Sydney with Red Cross friend Barbara Jenkinson, and her husband, Jeff. After touring Queensland and Sydney, Audrey and I flew to the Outback frontier, only to find that Alice Springs and Ayers Rock had become sophisticated tourist areas. I preferred the 1954 version.

Our stop in Rotorua, New Zealand, brought back many fond memories. We were hosted for several days by Rev. Bob Shuster, a local Maori leader, and by René Gillies, his granddaughter, who was head of education at the Rotorua Museum. We explored the steaming hot springs, enjoyed Maori culture, and went to the little Maori church. The outstanding experience was a day spent on a Maori sacred island where people camped, held ceremonies, women did weaving, and we ate in friendship. We entertained Bob and his family at a fond farewell dinner.

Return to Eastern Europe

In 2001, Patsy George and I arranged a home exchange with a young East German family from Leipzig. From there, social-work friend Richard Sullivan joined us to drive to the Czech Republic. At the Czech exit border we were told that we couldn't leave because we had no visas. We hadn't needed them to enter, but they wanted them for us to leave! Patsy argued that according to the travel flier she had read, these were not required. After she told the official, who continued to be abusive, that he didn't know his job, he insisted we two women wait in the car. When we stubbornly refused to pay a large fine, the official finally let us go.

We drove on to beautiful Budapest and then returned to Austria where I enjoyed memories of my honeymoon trip up the Danube and to haunts in Vienna. After Richard left us we visited East Berlin. Although I was tired, I enjoyed seeing the rubble that once was the Berlin Wall, which had separated families for decades.

South America

In 2003 my niece Cynthia invited her mother, Liz, and me on our first trip to South America. Cynthia had been doing research in Quito, Ecuador, and she arranged our tour. We stayed several days at the colonial home of the Arias family, which was now a hotel. Cynthia had been in love with Bernardo Arias, but they had decided to remain just friends. The two discussed their relationship over an extended family dinner, with Cynthia translating. When things got tense, our hosts' little granddaughter skipped around the table kissing everyone. While Bernardo's mother was disappointed that they would not marry, Liz was pleased.

At one point during that dinner, Liz haltingly explained to Bernardo's parents that I was a parliamentarian in the Canadian government. This news evoked murmurs of awe and approval. When Liz added the word "socialist," that was met with dead silence. Then Bernardo's father asked, "Marxist?" Both Liz and Cynthia rushed to explain, "No, social democrat—universal medicare, public education." That engendered a different response, an approving, "Ahhhh." So now, in some parts of Ecuador, I am probably known as the Mother of Medicare.

EPILOGUE

Summing Up

Where do I go from here? What is the relevance of this memoir and the lives that intertwined with mine? I think of the generation that has passed, or soon will. Although I am not religious, I begin to see a pattern that so often occurred, showing the continuity of life. When one person faces death, or dies, it seems to produce a positive replacement or compensation.

After I had a near-death illness, I recovered to lead an energetic and fulfilling life in the community and in politics. The night that Claude died, Ken's daughter Mariah was born, and my extended family took on new meaning. Betty and I became very close. When Pauline Jewett died, MPs Audrey McLaughlin, Dawn Black, Lynn Hunter and I all became very close friends. After my brother Ted died, Betty and I developed a new relationship with his wife, Kay. And after Betty died, my cousin Liz and her daughter Cynthia became an active part of my life. . . .

I became involved in politics because of my community work in Vancouver East and that was always my main interest and motivation. I really enjoyed people and wanted to see change that would bring greater equality, particularly for low-income people and women. Some politicians become involved in politics to gratify their egos and fulfill greater ambitions. For me that wasn't important. What was important was helping citizens gain more control over their lives. As their elected representative I helped to voice their concerns in Parliament. I opposed injustices and linked with people's movements across Canada and worldwide to bring about change.

Why did I choose and remain loyal to the NDP? From my university years onward, I felt the NDP reflected my values and goals. I like the collective democratic traditions and progressive policies developed by the CCF during the Depression and passed down from elders whom I admired. In Vancouver East, the NDP was the best party to represent struggling families, immigrants, the labour movement, unemployed people, and the elderly.

My background and focus was on social policies, but through the NDP I learned much more about how economics and capitalistic forces control resources, affect employment and influence decision-making, both inside and outside government. The NDP expanded my global concerns that had begun with my earlier travels. I strongly supported the UN and opposed war. Despite changing issues in four Parliaments, my commitment to the NDP remained strong. We didn't have to be in power to have influence. I believe our party has had a major impact, making Canada a country that cares for people, that appreciates our glorious environment, and that works for a better world.

Politics was personally satisfying and a lot of fun. I developed confidence and many new skills, and my outlook on life broadened. Our caucus was like a family (most of the time), and both Ed Broadbent and Audrey McLaughlin were great leaders with a strong sense of social democratic values. I especially enjoyed the sisterhood of women in the caucus, in the party, and the support of women across Canada. My interest in international issues expanded as I attended international conferences and travelled.

What I didn't like about politics was the entrenched, male-dominated culture of Parliament and the infighting within our caucus after a woman leader was elected. The media can be very cruel at times to women leaders and rarely recognize women politicians.

Cross-country flying is very stressful and is a special burden for west coast Members of Parliament. It is a lonely life in Ottawa and one rarely has time for family and old friends. I was lucky that Claude was so independent and so supportive.

As I grow older and have more time to be aware, I feel a connectedness with the environment—with the beauty of the Gulf Islands and False Creek and the marvels of our country, Canada. I look back at the potential of communities to support and stimulate people and to bring about change. And I realize the value of friends made—and often neglected—who are there when needed. Family has a new meaning as I watch a new generation grow. Politicians continue to squabble, but sometimes make progress. The global community calls out to me.

Yes, it has been a good life, and I have been privileged.

INDEX